D1094963

Francis Drake being "crowned" by the natives of New Albion (California) in June, 1579. (From Arnoldus Montanus, *Die unbekante neue Welt*; the Dapper issue, Amsterdam, 1673.)

FRANCIS DRAKE AND THE CALIFORNIA INDIANS, 1579

BY

ROBERT F. HEIZER

UNIVERSITY OF CALIFORNIA PRESS
BERKELEY AND LOS ANGELES
1947

University of California Publications in American Archaeology and Ethnology

Editors (Los Angeles): Ralph L. Beals, Franklin Fearing, Harry Hoijer

Volume 42, No. 3, pp. 251–302, plates 18–21, 1 figure in text, 2 illus.

Submitted by editors February 27, 1946

Issued Mardh 20, 1947

Price, cloth, $2.00; paper, $1.25

University of California Press

Berkeley and Los Angeles

California

————

Cambridge University Press

London, England

PRINTED IN THE UNITED STATES OF AMERICA

CONTENTS

FRANCIS DRAKE AND THE CALIFORNIA
INDIANS, 1579

BY

ROBERT F. HEIZER

GENERAL BACKGROUND

FOR NEARLY a century, historians, geographers, and anthropologists have attempted to solve the problem of locating Francis Drake's anchorage in California, but the opinion of no one investigator has been universally accepted. Indeed, it seems likely that the problem will forever remain insoluble in detail, although it may well be reduced to the possibility that one of two bays, either Drake's or Bodega, was the scene of Drake's stay in California.

Historically and ethnographically, Drake's California visit is exceedingly important. He was the first Englishman to see and describe the Indians of Upper California, and the third Caucasian to mention them. The account of the voyage given in *The World Encompassed by Sir Francis Drake* (London, 1628) (of uncertain authorship but usually attributed to Francis Fletcher) gives the earliest detailed description of California Indian life, including such particulars of native culture as ceremonial behavior and linguistic terms. This account is reproduced in Appendix II, below.

Historians and geographers have long since stated their reasons and qualifications for presenting certain conclusions about the location of Drake's anchorage, but anthropologists have never insisted vigorously enough that their contribution might be the most decisive of all in solving the problem. If it can be shown that the Indian language and culture described in the accounts of Drake's voyage to California are clearly those of one or another of the coastal Indian tribes, there will then be definite and unequivocal reasons for believing that in 1579 Drake landed on a part of the California coast inhabited by that tribe. Preliminary attempts at this type of solution have already been made, first by the greatest authority on the California Indians, Professor A. L. Kroeber,[1] and more recently by William W. Elmendorf and myself.[2]

In order to establish the background for the present study, it will be advisable to recapitulate the various opinions and claims. They may be listed under the headings: geographical, historical, and anthropological.

Geographical.—George C. Davidson, eminent and versatile scientist, first approached the problem of the location of Drake's California

---

[1] Alfred L. Kroeber, *Handbook of the Indians of California*, Bureau of American Ethnology, Bulletin 78 (Washington, D.C., 1925).
[2] Robert F. Heizer and William W. Elmendorf, "Francis Drake's California Anchorage in the Light of the Indian Language Spoken There," *Pacific Historical Review*, XI (1942), 213–217.

anchorage in 1858.[3] In the following years, as his familiarity with literary and cartographical sources expanded, he published other works,[4] and in 1908[5] he made his final statement. Davidson first thought that Drake's landfall had been in San Francisco Bay, but after more careful study he concluded that Drake's Bay was the anchorage (see pl. 20). Davidson's views have been carefully and critically reviewed by Henry R. Wagner[6] and J. W. Robertson.[7] Among other contributions relating to the problem of Drake's anchorage should be mentioned the works of Hubert Howe Bancroft[8] and the studies of Edward E. Hale,[9] as well as the searching analysis of Alexander G. McAdie and a more recent but similar paper by R. P. Bishop.[10]

Historical.—Although the trail was blazed by Davidson, it is Wagner who first claims our attention. He has concluded, after an exhaustive study of all available evidence, that Drake anchored first in Trinidad Bay and later in Bodega Bay. The harbor now called Drake's Bay was not, according to Wagner, the site of Drake's landfall in 1579. Robertson, next mentioned above, is the author of a critical review of previous "arguments advanced by certain historians in their selection of 'The Harbor of St. Francis.'"

Anthropological.—Wagner's major work on Drake bears abundant evidence that this historian, at least, is cognizant of the value of the ethnographic check method. However, he has not utilized all available documentary or ethnographic data to the fullest extent—a procedure of the utmost importance.

Davidson used the ethnographic method of solving the problem when he identified the Limantour Estero shellmound site with the Indian village depicted on the border map *Portus Novae Albionis* of the Jodocus

[3] George C. Davidson, "Directory for the Pacific Coast of the United States," *Report of the Superintendent of the Coast Survey . . . 1858* (Washington, D.C., 1859). App. 44, pp. 297–458.

[4] George C. Davidson, "An Examination of Some of the Early Voyages of Discovery and Exploration on the Northwest Coast of America from 1539 to 1603," *Report of the U.S. Coast and Geodetic Survey . . . June, 1886* (Washington, D.C., 1887), App. 7, pp. 155–253; and *Identification of Sir Francis Drake's Anchorage on the Coast of California in the Year 1579*, California Historical Society Publications (San Francisco, 1890).

[5] George C. Davidson, "Francis Drake on the Northwest Coast of America in the Year 1579. The Golden Hinde Did Not Anchor in the Bay of San Francisco," *Transactions and Proceedings of the Geographical Society of the Pacific*, ser. 2, Bull. 5.

[6] Henry R. Wagner, "George Davidson, Geographer of the Northwest Coast of America," *California Historical Society Quarterly*, XI (1932), 299–320. The idea that Drake entered San Francisco Bay was held by others than Davidson. See, for example, J. D. B. Stillman, "Did Drake Discover San Francisco Bay?" *Overland Monthly*, I (1868), 332–337. See also Henry R. Wagner, *Sir Francis Drake's Voyage around the World* (San Francisco, 1926), chaps. vii and viii, and notes on pp. 488–499, esp. pp. 495–496.

[7] J. W. Robertson, *The Harbor of St. Francis* (San Francisco, 1926).

[8] Hubert Howe Bancroft, *History of California*, Vol. I: *1542–1800* (San Francisco, 1884), pp. 81–94.

[9] Edward Everett Hale, in Justin Winsor, *Narrative and Critical History of the United States*, Vol. III, pp. 74–78.

[10] Alexander G. McAdie, "Nova Albion—1579," *Proceedings of the American Antiquarian Society*, n. s., XXVIII (1918), 189–198. R. P. Bishop, "Drake's Course in the North Pacific," *British Columbia Historical Quarterly*, III (1939), 151–182.

Hondius map *Vera totius expeditionis nauticae* (Amsterdam, 1590?)[11] and cited as evidence a tradition of the Nicasio Indians. In his day, many Coast Miwok Indians from Drake's Bay and Bodega Bay must have been still living. If at that time he had obtained from them the information which can no longer be found, owing to the extinction of the tribe, he would have performed an inestimable service.

In 1908, S. A. Barrett published his important work on Pomo ethnogeography in which he reproduced the California data on the voyage of Drake and made a brief evaluation.[12] After attempting a linguistic check with the word *Hioh* and directing attention to the feather-decorated baskets as Pomo-like, Barrett concludes that "these facts therefore point further to the tenability of the belief that Drake's landing was somewhere north of San Francisco bay, possibly even north of Point Reyes, though Pomo of the Southern and Southwestern dialectic area may have journeyed down to Drake's bay bringing their boat-shaped and ornamented baskets . . ."[13]

In Professor Kroeber's *Handbook of the Indians of California* there is an ethnographical analysis of a paraphrased version of *The World Encompassed*, together with an inquiry (more searching than that of Barrett's in 1908) into the identification of the words, such as *Hioh*, *Patah*, *Tobah*, and *Gnaah*, which appear in the Fletcher account.[14] Kroeber summarizes: "The ethnologist thus can only conclude that Drake summered on some piece of the coast not many miles north of San Francisco, and probably in the lagoon to which his name now attaches. He is assured that the recent native culture in this stretch existed in substantially the same form more than 300 years ago, and he has tolerable reason to believe that the Indians with whom the great explorer mingled were direct ancestors of the Coast Miwok."[15]

A verification of Kroeber's view has recently been presented in a short paper written by Heizer and Elmendorf[16] on the identification of the Indian words in the sixteenth-century accounts of Francis Fletcher and Richard Madox.[17] (Madox's account is reproduced in App. I, below.)

[11] F. P. Sprent, *Sir Francis Drake's Voyage round the World, 1577–1580, Two Contemporary Maps* (London, 1927), pp. 10–11, map 2.

[12] Samuel A. Barrett, *The Ethno-Geography of the Pomo and Neighboring Indians*, Univ. Calif. Publ. Am. Arch. and Ethn., Vol. 6, No. 1 (Berkeley, 1908), pp. 28–37.

[13] *Ibid.*, n. 7, pp. 36–37.

[14] Kroeber, *Handbook*, pp. 275–278.

[15] J. W. Robertson (*Francis Drake and Other Early Explorers along the Pacific Coast*, San Francisco, 1927), in discussing Kroeber's analysis of the Fletcher account (*op. cit.*, p. 177), says: "There seems to be no proof either that Drake landed at any particular harbor, or that anything can be adduced so specific as to establish his residence on this coast." The latter part of this statement cannot be maintained seriously in the face of Kroeber's presentation of direct evidence to the contrary.

[16] Heizer and Elmendorf, "Francis Drake's California Anchorage."

[17] The words recorded by Fletcher are in *The World Encompassed*. The Madox vocabulary was printed by E. G. R. Taylor, "Francis Drake and the Pacific," *Pacific Historical Review*, I (1932), 360–369. Madox's account has been further discussed by Wagner in the *California Historical Society Quarterly*, XI (1932), 309–311.

In this paper it is shown that Drake must have landed in territory occupied by the Coast Miwok-speaking natives (fig. 1), but the exact location of his landing is not positively indicated since there are four bays along Coast Miwok territory in which Drake might conceivably

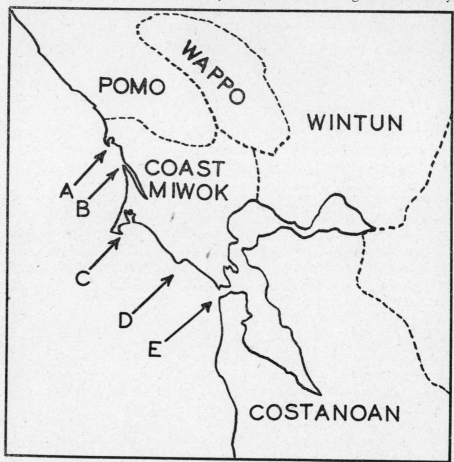

Fig. 1. Location of west-central California Indian linguistic groups. A, Bodega Bay; B, Tomales Bay; C, Drake's Bay; D, Bolinas Bay; E, San Francisco Bay.

have anchored.[18] Of these four bays, Bolinas, Drake's, Tomales, and Bodega, only two, Drake's and Bodega, can be considered seriously.

A final piece of evidence, this time archaeological, has recently come to light in the plate of brass left by Drake in 1579. This plate was originally found at Laguna Ranch (pl. 21) on Drake's Bay in 1934 (?),[19] was moved elsewhere, and was rediscovered in 1936.[20] Although some

[18] See Barrett, *Ethno-Geography*, map facing p. 332, and Kroeber, *Handbook*, fig. 22, p. 274, for the area held by the Coast Miwok.
[19] For details see *California Historical Society Quarterly*, XVI (1937), 192.
[20] For particulars see *Drake's Plate of Brass: Evidence of His Visit to California in 1579*, California Historical Society, Special Publication No. 13 (San Francisco, 1937).

skeptics have questioned the genuineness of the plate of brass,[21] they have not altered the facts establishing the plate's authenticity as shown by the investigations of such scholars as Allen Chickering,[22] Professor Herbert E. Bolton,[23] and Drs. Fink and Polushkin.[24] Consequently, the problem of Drake's anchorage is nearer solution. Although the plate is a portable object, it was probably not carried far. It could have been carried to Drake's Bay from Bodega Bay; but, on the other hand, it could always have been at Drake's Bay. In the absence of evidence that it was moved early in its history, it may not be claiming overmuch to assume that the post with the plate of brass was originally erected in Drake's Bay.

So much, then, for an abbreviated review of the opinions on the location of Francis Drake's California anchorage. Arguments have been advanced, by other students, that Drake anchored in Trinidad, Bodega, or Drake's Bay. It is my purpose here to analyze, as carefully as possible, the ethnographic data contained in Francis Fletcher's account in *The World Encompassed*, with the hope of determining in which of these bays Drake actually stayed in June, 1579. The Trinidad Bay landfall theory will first be investigated, in an attempt to determine whether the Indians mentioned in Fletcher's account are identifiable with the Yurok tribe which, in historic times, occupied this territory.

The Trinidad Bay Landfall Theory

Henry R. Wagner is the chief proponent of the Trinidad Bay theory, and bases his conclusion upon two lines of evidence, (1) cartographical and (2) ethnographical.[25] The Jodocus Hondius map, with a small inset of the *Portus Novae Albionis*, does resemble Trinidad Harbor, but since all admit that the Hondius "Portus" is imperfectly drawn, and only generally impressionistic, it can hardly be maintained that it resembles less the outline of Bodega Bay or Drake's Bay. Wagner points out that there was a Yurok village near the spot indicated on the Hondius map as occu-

---

[21] See R. B. Haselden, "Is the Drake Plate of Brass Genuine?" *California Historical Society Quarterly*, XVI (1937), 271–274. Haselden's queries have been answered already. W. Hume-Rotherby (review of *Drake's Plate of Brass Authenticated*, in *Geographical Journal*, CXIV [1939], 54–55) points out that the letters engraved on the plate (B, N, M) are not paralleled by other sixteenth-century inscriptions, and that the form of the numeral 5 is suspect. These and other problems which he poses have the effect of creating a smokescreen of doubt without contributing anything new. Wagner is skeptical of the date on the plate (June 17) and of the fact that the plate is of brass rather than lead ("Creation of Rights of Sovereignty through Symbolic Acts," *Pacific Historical Review*, VII [1938], 297–326).

[22] Allen L. Chickering, "Some Notes with Regard to Drake's Plate of Brass," *California Historical Society Quarterly*, XVI (1937), 275–281, and "Further Notes on the Drake Plate," *ibid.*, XVIII (1939), 251–253.

[23] Herbert E. Bolton, "Francis Drake's Plate of Brass," in *Drake's Plate of Brass*, California Historical Society, Special Publication No. 13 (San Francisco, 1937).

[24] C. G. Fink and E. P. Polushkin, *Drake's Plate of Brass Authenticated* . . . California Historical Society, Special Publication No. 14 (San Francisco, 1938).

[25] Wagner's theory is not stated explicitly in any one place, hence specific reference is impossible. See his *Sir Francis Drake's Voyage around the World* (San Francisco, 1926), pp. 156–158, 169.

pied by an Indian town.[26] But in Drake's Bay and Bodega Bay, the outlines of which also resemble that of the *Portus Novae Albionis*, there are also Indian shellmounds in about the same relative position as the village shown on the Hondius map.

Fletcher's reference to a "canow" has led Wagner to identify this with the Yurok dugout log canoe. If Fletcher's "canow" were described in any detail, it would settle the problem of whether it meant a Yurok dugout log canoe or a Coast Miwok tule *balsa* such as was used in Drake's or Bodega Bay. Kroeber has also commented upon this unenlightening word, saying, "Either custom changed after Drake's day, or his canoe is a loose term for the tule *balsa* which was often boat-shaped, with raised sides, especially when intended for navigation." Wagner says in answer, "To this it may be objected that . . . tule *balsas* were in use in Drake's Bay in 1595 and were so recognized without difficulty." They were recognized indeed, *but by a Spanish sailor already familiar with the type*. Fletcher in his offhand manner dismissed the native boat with a word which *he* was familiar with. Perhaps the strongest argument in favor of identifying Fletcher's "canow" as a tule *balsa* lies in the fact that he states that a single person came out to the *Golden Hinde*. If it had been a Yurok dugout, and particularly in the open bay of Trinidad, one man could not have managed the canoe. For example, the Bruno de Hezeta account of Trinidad Bay in 1775 states: "Before they [the Spaniards] drew near the land to drop anchor four canoes carrying twenty-four men came out to receive them. They drew near the ships and were given food and beads, with which they went away without fear . . ."[27] It might also be worth noting that Fletcher states that the person in the canoe remained "at a reasonable distance staying himself," and would accept only a hat, "refusing vtterly to meddle with any other thing . . . ." One other account may be cited to support the identification of the "canow" with the *balsa*. Sebastián Cermeño, in 1595 at Drake's Bay, wrote, ". . . many Indians appeared on the beach and soon *one of them* got into a small craft which they employ, like a çacate of the lake of Mexico."[28]

By inference, the native house described by Fletcher has been identified as a Yurok house. I do not think this claim will hold, since the house in Fletcher's account is described as semisubterranean, circular, conical-roofed, covered with earth, and with a roof entrance, whereas the Yurok

---

[26] This is shown even more clearly on the Hezeta map of 1775 reproduced by Herbert E. Bolton, *Historical Memoirs of New California by Fray Francisco Palóu*, 4 vols. (Berkeley, 1926), Vol. IV, facing p. 16. George C. Davidson in his *Identification* (pp. 17–18, 34, 39) made a similar identification of the Indian village site at the Limantour Estero in Drake's Bay.

[27] Bolton, *op. cit.*, n. 19. See also L. L. Loud, *Ethnogeography and Archaeology of the Wiyot Territory*, Univ. Calif. Publ. Am. Arch. and Ethn., Vol. 14, No. 3 (Berkeley, 1918), p. 243.

[28] H. R. Wagner, *Spanish Voyages to the Northwest Coast of America*, California Historical Society, Special Publication No. 4 (San Francisco, 1929), p. 158.

dwelling (*not* the sweathouse), built wholly of planks, is rectangular, is a surface structure except for an interior rectangular pit, has a round door entering just above the ground and through the side wall, and bears a double-ridged roof with two slopes.[29] Thus, the house described by Fletcher cannot be a Yurok house of Trinidad Bay. On the other hand, as will be shown in detail later, the house described by Fletcher is the central California earth-covered dwelling, typical of the Coast Miwok of Drake's Bay and Bodega Bay.

Wagner, in his attempt to show that Drake landed at Trinidad Bay, makes a further point. He says:"An additional indication that Drake was in this bay [Trinidad] may be gleaned from the finding there of knives in 1775 by Bruno Heceta . . . It seems probable, then, that the knives found at Trinidad by Heceta were relics of Drake's expedition."[30] It is scarcely credible that numbers of iron knives, sword blades, and such implements could have been preserved through two centuries of use. Since the wooden-sheathed knives were expressly stated to be ill-made, and in view of Fray Miguel de la Campa's statement in 1775 that "one of them [i.e., one of the Indians] made his [knife] from a nail which he had found in a piece of wreckage and had beaten out with a stone,"[31] it is more than likely that the Trinidad Indians' knives were pounded out of pieces of iron found imbedded in local sea-borne wreckage.[32] Logic and probability lead inevitably to the conclusion that there is nothing in the fact that knives were found at Trinidad Bay in 1775 from which to suspect or to postulate Drake's presence in that place two centuries earlier.

Now for a brief comparison of some specific Indian culture elements and examples of the language, as reported in *The World Encompassed* and in Richard Madox's narrative, with those of Yurok Indian culture. Madox was chaplain on Edward Fenton's expedition of 1582, and in his diary are some notes on California which he jotted down after conversation with some members of the crew which had sailed with Drake two years earlier.

The flat shell disk beads of the account are not an element of Yurok material culture. The standard Yurok shell bead is the hollow tusk shell (*Dentalia indianorum*), which is long, cylindrical, and of small diameter. The feathered net caps may possibly find cognates in the flicker headbands of the Yurok, though these bands were known over the whole

[29] For details see Kroeber, *Handbook*, pp. 78–79, pl. 9; and Loud, *Ethnogeography*, pp. 243, 244.
[30] Wagner, *Drake's Voyage*, pp. 157, 158.
[31] "Fray Benito de la Sierra's Account of the Hezeta Expedition to the Northwest Coast in 1775," trans. by A. J. Baker, introd. and notes by H. R. Wagner, *California Historical Society Quarterly*, IX (1930), 218.
[32] See T. A. Rickard, "The Use of Iron and Copper by the Indians of British Columbia," *British Columbia Historical Quarterly*, III (1939), 26–27, where the Hezeta finds are expressly discussed. Rickard's opinion also differs from Wagner's.

of interior and coastal California (cf. pl. 18, *a*). The feathered baskets, however, cannot possibly be Yurok, since their manufacture and use is restricted to the Pomo-Miwok-Wappo tribes which lived far to the south of the Yurok. The "canow" of Fletcher, as had been pointed out, can hardly be equated with the heavy Yurok river- and ocean-going dugout canoe. This brief comparison should be convincing evidence that Drake's chronicler did not describe the Trinidad Bay Yurok; but there is added evidence in the word forms of the Madox vocabulary. Madox gives "bread" as *Cheepe*, which the Yurok render *pop-sho*. "Sing" is given as *Gnaah* in *The World Encompassed*, the Yurok word being *wer-o-rur*. "Chief" is given by Fletcher and Madox as *Hioh* or *Hioghe*, the Yurok word being *si-at-lau*.

The decision of whether or not Drake entered Trinidad Bay, which is not convenient as a port, and is, moreover, rock-studded,[33] must rest in part upon a study of the Hondius *Portus Novae Albionis*, of which, Wagner says, ". . . perhaps a very close approximation to the actual configuration of the bay [in which Drake anchored] cannot be expected." Certainly the native customs, houses, and language do not offer the slightest support to the theory that Drake observed the Yurok Indians.[34]

THE ARGUMENTS FOR THE BODEGA BAY OR DRAKE'S BAY LANDFALL

Wagner, then, has attempted to prove that Drake landed in Bodega Bay; Davidson and McAdie, that he anchored in Drake's Bay; whereas Kroeber, Heizer and Elmendorf, Barrett, and Bancroft failed to reach a decision on which bay gave anchorage to the *Golden Hinde*.

In the following pages I shall analyze by comparative ethnographic technique the cultural data relating to the California Indians as given in the several accounts of the Drake visit in 1579. These sources are:

1. The *World Encompassed* account, which I judge to be the fullest and most reliable.[35]

2. The *Famous Voyage* account, which is abbreviated and therefore less complete in detail.[36]

3. The second declaration of John Drake (1582), a brief independent account of the occurrences in California (see below, App. I).[37]

---

[33] Francisco Eliza in 1793 said: "The Puerto de Trinidad is quite small; no vessel can be moored so as to turn with the wind or tide. The bottom for the most part is rock. The land consists of quite high and extended hills full of pines and oaks" (H. R. Wagner, "The Last Spanish Exploration of the Northwest Coast and the Attempt to Colonize Bodega Bay," *California Historical Society Quarterly*, X [1931], 335). For photographic views of Trinidad Bay see Thomas T. Waterman, *Yurok Geography*, Univ. Calif. Publ. Am. Arch. and Ethn., Vol. XVI, No. 5 (Berkeley, 1920), pls. 1, 16.

[34] Kroeber, *Handbook*, p. 278, inferentially concurs with this conclusion.

[35] Reprinted in *Drake's Plate of Brass*, pp. 32–46.

[36] Reprinted in *Drake's Plate of Brass*, pp. 27–30, and by Wagner in *Drake's Voyage*, pp. 274–277.

[37] Printed in Zelia Nuttall, *New Light on Drake*, Hakluyt Society, ser. 2, Vol. 34 (London, 1914), pp. 50–51.

4. Richard Madox's notes on "Ships Land" (New Albion), which contain a revealing vocabulary of the Indian language.[38]

An exhaustive ethnography of the Coast Miwok has never been published. The main sources of Coast Miwok ethnography used in this paper may be enumerated as follows:

1. Data contained in various historical accounts. These are, for the most part, incidental data and are not, even in total amount, extensive. The accounts will be cited at the appropriate places below.

2. Published ethnographic notes such as are given in S. A. Barrett's *The Ethno-Geography of the Pomo and Neighboring Indians*, A. L. Kroeber's *Handbook of the Indians of California*, and many others which likewise will be cited below.

3. The extensive manuscript notes on the Coast Miwok in the possession of Dr. Isabel Kelly. Dr. Kelly has kindly lent her material for the purpose of checking ethnographic items.

ANALYSIS OF THE WORLD ENCOMPASSED ACCOUNT

On June 17 (Old Style), Drake's ship entered "a conuenient and fit harborough." The next day, "the people of the countrey shewed themselues; sending off a man with great expedition to vs in a canow." On the 21st, the ship was brought near shore, her goods were landed, and defense works were erected. Numbers of natives made their appearance for a brief time, then returned to their homes in a near-by village. At the end of two days (June 23), during which no natives had been seen, there appeared "a great assembly of men, women, and children." As the narrator says, the local people seen on the 23d had probably "dispersed themselues into the country, to make knowne the newes. . . ." There follows in the narrative a long and detailed account of the activities of the natives who remained assembled near the camp of the English. Finally, after three more days (the account says June 26), word of the strange newcomers had spread even further, and there "were assembled the greatest number of people, which wee could reasonably imagine, to dwell within any conuenient distance round about." Among these were the "king," the *Hioh* of the Indians, and "his guard, of about 100. tall and warlike men."

This sequence of visits is of some interest. If Drake landed at Drake's Bay, the natives seen by him on June 18 and 21 were certainly local Coast Miwok living close at hand around the bay. The influx of people

---

[38] As Barrett (*Ethno-Geography*, map at end), Kroeber (*Handbook*, pp. 272–275), and C. H. Merriam ("Distribution and Classification of the Mewan Stock in California," *American Anthropologist*, IX [1907], 338–357), show, the Coast Miwok inhabited both Bodega Bay and Drake's Bay territory. Thus the language (except for minor dialectic differentiation) and culture are undoubtedly very similar at both bays. This makes the problem of exclusive selection somewhat difficult. The Madox vocabulary (see below, p. 282) was first presented in E. G. R. Taylor, "Francis Drake and the Pacific: Two Fragments," *Pacific Historical Review*, I (1932), 360–369.

on the 23d probably means that they were drawn from relatively near-by Coast Miwok villages—from near Olema, or from both shores of Tomales Bay. But even larger crowds of natives came on the 26th, and among them were the *Hioh* and his retinue. The group arriving on the 26th probably came from some distance. If this crowd gathered at Drake's Bay, they could well have been recruited from Bodega Bay, and possibly included a number of Southern Pomo neighbors. The elapsed time (i.e., between June 21 and June 26) can be readily accounted for by two factors: (1) time for communication to be established from Drake's to Bodega Bay and for the return of the Bodega people, and (2) time for convocation of the group, decision on a plan of action, and preparation for the elaborate ceremony performed at the English camp on the 26th.

If, however, Drake landed in Bodega Bay, the situation would be somewhat different. The visitors of the 18th and 21st would be Bodega Coast Miwok. Those arriving on the 23d could have been Tomales Bay or Olema Coast Miwok, and the arrival on the 26th of the *Hioh* with his retinue and followers might mark the presence of Southern Pomo, or, less probably, Central Pomo who were concentrated in the interior some fifty miles north of Bodega Bay.

It is credible, then, that Drake landed in either Drake's Bay or Bodega Bay, since the native words listed by Fletcher and Madox all belong to the Coast Miwok language and not to any Pomo dialect.[39] It is improbable that the ceremonies, customs, and material culture forms described by Fletcher can be *specifically* attributed to the Pomo, as intimated by Wagner,[40] for at least three reasons: (1) Northern Coast Miwok and Southern Pomo cultures are practically indistinguishable; (2) the words *Hioh* and *Gnaah* seem to be Coast Miwok words rather than words of Pomo attribution; and (3) if Drake landed in Coast Miwok territory it is unlikely that the Pomo would be permitted to enter the territory of their southern neighbors and to perform a ceremony which the Coast Miwok themselves were as well able to do.

Following is an examination of the day-by-day account of Fletcher.

June 18.—A single man in a "canow" (probably a tule *balsa*) came out to the ship and delivered an oration. The canoeman also brought with him, and threw into the ship, a bunch of black feathers tied in a round bundle, and a small basket filled with an herb ("Tobah"), both of which were tied to a short stick.

In 1595, Sebastián Cermeño noted almost exactly the same thing in

---

[39] The Fletcher-Madox vocabulary list does not resemble the Yurok words for the same items or phrases.

[40] Wagner, *Drake's Voyage*, p. 147. B. Aginsky ("Psychopathic Trends in Culture," *Character and Personality*, VII [1939], 331–343) quotes Fletcher's description of Indian weeping and self-laceration, and calls them Pomo, asserting that Drake landed in their territory and that the ceremonies given in honor of the English exemplify the "Dionysian" phase of Pomo culture.

Drake's Bay,[41] and something very similar was observed by Francisco Mourelle in Bodega Bay in 1775.[42] Cermeño says: "On the day on which the ship anchored in the bay, about four o'clock in the afternoon, many Indians appeared on the beach and soon one of them got into a small craft which they employ like a çacate of the lake of Mexico. He came off to the ship, where he remained quite a time talking in his language, no one understanding what he said." Mourelle's statement is similar: there is no mention of a speech by the Indians in "tule canoes," but they presented the Spanish with plumes of feathers, "bone rosaries" (shell bead necklaces?), garlands of feathers which they wore around their heads, and a canister of seeds which tasted like walnuts.

The feather bundle cannot be specifically identified, but it may be the ceremonial black feather bundle (pl. 18, *b*) most often associated with the central California Kuksu cult. Some of these have been illustrated by Professor Kroeber[43] and R. B. Dixon.[44] The small basket filled with the herb called *Tobah* or *Tabah* has led some students to identify this herb as tobacco (*Nicotiana* sp.) John P. Harrington quotes the sections from *The World Encompassed* which contain mention of *Tabah* or *Tobah*, and assumes that the word has reference to tobacco (*Nicotiana bigelovii*).[45] Upon what grounds he identifies the herb mentioned by Fletcher as tobacco is not stated, since the local words for tobacco are different,[46] nor is it stated in the account that the herb was smoked. Wagner doubts that the herb called *Tobah* was tobacco, and in this he and I are in agreement. It cannot be determined whether or not a *Nicotiana* was referred to by Fletcher, nor is it likely that this question will ever be settled. What does seem clear is that "Tobah" is not an Indian word, but the name applied to the herb by the English narrator.[47] This supposition is enhanced by the fact that *The Famous Voyage* mentions the herb by the name "tabacco," a word already known in England before Drake started on his voyage around the world.[48] It may be concluded that Fletcher's word "Tobah" or "Tabah" comes from the English word "tabacco," "tobacco," "tabaco," and is not a California

[41] Wagner, *Spanish Voyages*, p. 158.

[42] Don Francisco Mourelle, "Journal of a Voyage in 1775 to explore the Coast of America, Northward of California ... ," in *Miscellanies of the Honorable Daines Barrington* (London, 1781), pp. 471*–534*. See also Wagner, *Drake's Voyage*, p. 158.

[43] Kroeber. *Handbook*, fig. 21.

[44] Roland B. Dixon, "The Northern Maidu," *Bulletin of the American Museum of Natural History*, Vol. XVII, Pt. III (1905), fig. 19.

[45] John P. Harrington, "Tobacco among the Karuk Indians," Bureau of American Ethnology, Bull. 94 (1932), 17–18, 40.

[46] The Coast Miwok word for tobacco is *kaiyau*. For the North, Central, Eastern, and Northeastern Pomo it is *saxa, saka, sako:* for the Southern, Southwestern, and Southeastern Pomo it is *kawa, tom-kawa* (Roland B. Dixon, "Words for Tobacco in American Indian Languages," *American Anthropologist*, XXIII [1921], 30).

[47] See discussion in Heizer and Elmendorf, "Francis Drake's California Anchorage."

[48] Berthold Laufer, "Introduction of Tobacco into Europe," Field Museum of Natural History Anthropological Leaflet No. 19 (1924), pp. 6 ff.

Indian word. In this conclusion I am in agreement with Professor Kroeber.[49]

June 18–21.—There is no mention of Indians between the 18th and the 21st of June. After referring to the man in the "canow," Fletcher continues, "After which time, our boate could row no way, but wondring at vs as at gods, they would follow the same with admiration." This would indicate that June 19 and 20 were spent exploring the bay in a small boat to discover a proper spot for careening the treasure-laden ship, which had sprung a leak at sea.

June 21.—On this day the ship was brought near shore and anchored. Goods were landed, and some sort of stone fortification was erected for defense. The Indians made their appearance in increasing numbers until there was a "great number both of men and women." It is clearly apparent that the natives were not simply curious, but acted, as Fletcher points out, "as men rauished in their mindes" and "their errand being rather with submission and feare to worship vs as Gods, then to haue any warre with vs as with mortall men." It would seem that the natives demonstrated clearly their fear and wonderment at the English, and it is certain that they behaved as no other natives had done in the experience of the chronicler. The English gave their visitors shirts and linen cloth, in return for which (as Fletcher thought) the Indians presented to Drake and some of the English such things as feathers, net caps, quivers for arrows, and animal skins which the women wore. Then, having visited for a time, the natives left for their homes about three-quarters of a mile away. As soon as they were home, the Indians began to lament, "extending their voices, in a most miserable and dolefull manner of shreeking." Inserted between the passages dealing with the departure of the Indians to their homes and their lamenting is a description of their houses and dress. The houses are described as "digged round within the earth, and haue from the vppermost brimmes of the circle, clefts of wood set vp, and ioyned close together at the top, like our spires on the steeple of a church: which being couered with earth, suffer no water to enter, and are very warme, the doore in the most part of them, performes the office of a chimney, to let out the smoake: its made in bignesse and fashion, like to an ordinary scuttle in a ship, and standing slopewise: their beds are the hard ground, onely with rushes strewed vpon it, and lying round about the house, haue their fire in the middest . . ." The men for the most part were naked, and the women wore a shredded bulrush (tule? *Scirpus* sp.) skirt which hung around the hips. Women also wore a shoulder cape of deerskin with the hair upon it.

From the foregoing facts some important conclusions can be drawn.

[49] *Handbook*, p. 277.

Another representation of the "crowning" of Francis Drake. (From an old engraving; provenience not known.)

First, the wonderment of the natives is but an extension of attitudes they had daily shown from the 17th to the 20th; and similar manifestations continued throughout the long stay of the English.[50] The English were looked upon as unusual, perhaps supernatural, visitors, since nothing is more clear than the fact that they were not treated as ordinary mortals. Kroeber has suggested that the Indians regarded the English as the returned dead, and there is much to be said for this view, as will be shown later. The doleful shrieking, weeping, and crying are evidence *sui generis* that the presence of the English was in some way associated with ghosts or the dead.[51]

The circular semisubterranean house, roofed over with poles and earth-covered, is also characteristic of a wide area of central California. The Coast Miwok of Drake's Bay and Bodega Bay[52] used these houses, as did the Pomo.[53] It is clearly not a temporary brush-covered house like those seen in the Bodega–Tomales Bay region.[54] The "caules of network" undoubtedly refer to the well-known net caps of central California,[55] a type so widespread that exact localization or provenience is impossible.

The Fletcher account is fairly specific on particulars of dress—women wore shredded bulrush skirts and deerskin shoulder capes, and men were ordinarily naked. The bulrush or tule-fiber clothing is attested for

[50] Compare Fletcher's statements of the attitude of the Indians with that of Cermeño, who was in Drake's Bay in 1595 and said, ". . . the other Indians approached in an humble manner and as if terrorized, and yielded peacefully" (Wagner, *Spanish Voyages*, p. 159).

[51] This custom is a general central Californian cultural feature. See E. M. Loeb, *Pomo Folkways*, Univ. Calif. Publ. Am. Arch. and Ethn., Vol. XIX, No. 2 (Berkeley, 1926), pp. 286, 287, 291; R. B. Dixon, "The Northern Maidu," pp. 242, 252; A. L. Kroeber, *The Patwin and their Neighbors*, Univ. Calif. Publ. Am. Arch. and Ethn., Vol. XXIX, No. 4 (Berkeley, 1932) p. 272; C. Purdy, "The Pomo Indian Baskets and Their Makers," *Overland Monthly*, XV (1901), 449. See also below, notes 56 and 57.

[52] Dixon, "The Northern Maidu," fig. 33.

[53] Fritz Krause, *Die Kultur der Kalifornischen Indianer* (Leipzig, 1921), map 4.

[54] A rather lengthy digression must be made here since the details are involved. S. A. Barrett ("Pomo Buildings," *Holmes Anniversary Volume*, Washington, D.C., 1916, p. 7) states that semisubterranean, earth-covered houses were used about 1900 by men of means (chiefs, good hunters, lucky gamblers, and medicine men). This house was a small edition of the larger dance house (described by Barrett, *Ethno-Geography*, p. 10). Fletcher's description says that in the majority of houses the combined roof entrance and smoke hole was present. This qualification does not exclude the possibility that some houses had the ground-level tunnel entrance which should be expected in the area. In historic times the Pomo seem, in large part, to have given up making these permanent dwellings in favor of less permanent mat- or grass-covered houses, which were inexpensive and more convenient to erect. The same process of loss seems to have occurred among the Coast Miwok, since Dr. Kelly's informants did not remember such houses. Archaeological sites in the Point Reyes–Drake's Bay region show numerous circular depressions which are clearly the remains of such houses. A further indication of their presence at an earlier time can be gained from "linguistic archaeology." The Sierra (Interior) Miwok use the word *kotca* for the earth-covered, underground house with combined roof entrance and smoke hole (S. A. Barrett and E. W. Gifford, "Miwok Material Culture," *Bulletin of the Public Museum of the City of Milwaukee*, Vol. II, No. 4 [1933], p. 198). The same word for house (i.e., dwelling) is present among the Coast Miwok (Barrett, *Ethno-Geography*, word no. 64, p. 71), who once had a similar house, as is shown by archaeological remains, but abandoned it in ethnographic times. It is not unreasonable on these grounds to assume the presence in Coast Miwok territory of the type of house described by Fletcher.

[55] Wagner, "The Last Spanish Exploration of the Northwest Coast and the Attempt to Colonize Bodega Bay," *California Historical Society Quarterly*, X (1931), 331.

Bodega Bay[56] and Drake's Bay,[57] but it is also found generally throughout central California. Men were generally naked in California, so Fletcher does not note here a distinctive cultural trait. The wearing of deerskin capes by the women is not strictly substantiated by the observations of later explorers, although Cermeño (1595) said that the women in Drake's Bay "covered their private parts with straw and skins of animals."[58] Archibald Menzies noted that the women in Tomales Bay wore a deerskin wrapped around their middle and reaching to the knees,[59] and Francisco Eliza said that near Bodega Bay "the women cover themselves from the waist down with deer skins."[60] Colnett mentions the Indian dress of deerskins in Bodega Bay.[61]

June 23.—On this day, after a two-day absence, "a great assembly of men, women, and children" appeared at the camp of the English. The Indians stopped at the top of the hill at the bottom of which Drake's camp was pitched, and one man made "a long and tedious oration: deliuered with strange and violent gestures, his voice being extended to the vttermost strength of nature . . ." At the conclusion of the speech or oration, all the other Indians reverently bowed their bodies "in a dreaming manner" (?) and cried *"Oh"* in approbation. Then the men, leaving their bows, women, and children behind them, came down to the English with presents and gifts. While the men were gift giving, the women cried and shrieked piteously, tore their cheeks with their fingernails until the blood flowed, tore off the single covering from the upper parts of the body, and, holding their hands high, cast themselves on the ground with great violence, regardless of consequences. The English, grieved at this spectacle of sacrifice, attempted to dissuade the Indians by praying and indicating by signs that their God lived above. During this "performance" (prayers, singing Psalms, and reading chapters of the Bible), the Indians "sate very attentiuely: and obseruing the end of euery pause, with one voice still cryed, Oh, greatly reioycing in our exercises." The natives were watching with great interest what seemed to them a ceremonial performance (which it actually was, but not in the sense in which the Indians understood it). The singing of Psalms interested the Indians most, and whenever the natives came, says Fletcher, their first request was *Gnaah*, an entreaty that the English should sing. After the Indians and English had exchanged ceremonial performances

---

[56] Bolton, *Historical Memoirs of New California by Fray Francisco Palóu*, Vol. IV, p. 48.

[57] I. T. Kelly, "Coast Miwok Ethnography." (MS).

[58] Wagner, *Spanish Voyages*, p. 158. J. Broughton, in his *Voyage of Discovery to the North Pacific Ocean . . . in the Years 1795 . . . 1798* (London, 1804), said that the Drake's Bay Indian men whom he saw were naked, but that the women were clothed "in some degree."

[59] "Menzies' California Journal," ed. by Alice Eastwood, *California Historical Society Quarterly*, II (1924), 302–303.

[60] Wagner, "The Last Spanish Exploration," p. 331.

[61] James Colnett, *The Journal of Captain James Colnett aboard the "Argonaut" from April 26, 1789 to November 3, 1791*, ed. by F. N. Howay, Champlain Society, Publ. No. 26 (Toronto, 1940), p. 175.

of a religious nature, the Indians again departed, giving back to the English everything they had received.

The oration by the man at the top of the hill may perhaps be likened to a speech that Cermeño made note of, when, in 1595, he was at Drake's Bay: ". . . Indians from near by kept coming and the chief talked a long time."[62] It is not improbable that the speaker mentioned by Fletcher was a messenger dispatched to announce the later coming of the big chief.[63] Or, the orator may simply have been a local village chief who delivered a long address or salutation to the English. The existence, at least, of such orators is known.[64] The signal of approbation, "Oh," has already been remarked upon by S. A. Barrett: "The expressions of assent and pleasure which are here noted are those commonly used not only by the Moqueluman Coast Miwok peoples of this region but by the Pomo to the north where such expressions as *o, yo, iyo*, varying with the locality, are heard, as evidences of approval of the sentiment expressed by the speaker, or of satisfaction with the performance of a dance."[65] When the preliminaries were over, the men came down the hill, and the women remained behind, lamenting, and lacerating their flesh. Crying and tearing the cheeks with the fingernails, as an ethnographic practice in connection with mourning, is documented for the Coast Miwok[66] and Pomo.[67] The word *Gnaah*, by which (so Fletcher states) the Indians asked the English to sing, can possibly be likened to the Coast Miwok *koyá*, "sing."[68] If it is granted that *Gnaah* is equivalent to *koyá*, there is good reason to believe that Coast Miwok were the main frequenters of Drake's camp, since Fletcher says, ". . . whensoever they resorted to vs, their first request was *Gnaah*, by which they intreated that we would sing." The words for "sing" in neighboring Indian tongues are so unlike *Gnaah* that no idea of connection can be entertained.

June 26.—After three days, there "were assembled the greatest num-

---

[62] Wagner, *Spanish Voyages*, p. 159.

[63] Exact documentation is impossible here, but such an explanation would fit the facts, and the custom of sending a messenger to announce a visit was a feature of the whole area (Loeb, *Pomo Folkways*, p. 49).

[64] See E. W. Gifford and A. L. Kroeber. *Culture Element Distributions, IV: Pomo*, Univ. Calif. Publ. Am. Arch. and Ethn., Vol. XXXVII, No. 4 (Berkeley, 1937), elements nos. 805–807, p. 154.

[65] Barrett, *Ethno-Geography*, p. 415.

[66] Kelly, "Coast Miwok Ethnography."

[67] Stephen Powers, *Tribes of California* (Washington, D.C., 1877), pp. 165, 169, 170, 181); Loeb, *Pomo Folkways*, pp. 286, 287; Barrett, "Pomo Buildings," p. 11. See also above, p. 261, n. 42. I can see no possible relationship between the clear account by Fletcher of self-laceration and Wagner's discussion of tattooing (*Drake's Voyage*, p. 494, n. 49). As the comparative notes cited clearly show, the tearing of the flesh by the California Indians is no "story" which needs an involved, roundabout, and improbable explanation.

[68] For the Coast Miwok and Pomo words for "sing" see Barrett, *Ethno-Geography*, word no. 265, pp. 67, 79. The Pomo words are totally unlike *Gnaah* or *koyá*. See also Heizer and Elmendorf, "Francis Drake's California Anchorage," pp. 214, 216. There is a logical possibility of a copying error in *Gnaah* from Fletcher's manuscript notes. If it had originally been written *Guaah* or *Gyaah*, it would be very close indeed to *koyá*.

ber of people which wee could reasonably imagine to dwell within any conuenient distance round about." Included in the crowd were the "king" and his "guard" of about one hundred men. Before the king showed himself, two "Embassadors or messengers" appeared, to announce his coming and to ask for a present "as a token that his comming might be in peace." Drake complied, and soon the "king with all his traine came forward." The king and his retinue "cryed continually after a singing manner" as they came, but as they approached nearer they strove to "behaue themselues with a certaine comelinesse and grauity in all their actions." In the front of the procession came a man bearing the "Septer or royall mace," a black stick about four and a half feet long, to which were tied long, looped strings of shell disk beads, and two "crownes," a larger and a smaller, made of knitwork and covered with a pattern of colored feathers. Only a few men were seen to wear the disk bead necklaces ("chaines"). Fletcher observes that in proportion to the number of "chaines" a man wears, "as some ten, some twelve, some twentie, and as they exceed in number of chaines, so are they thereby knowne to be the more honorable personages." Next to the scepter bearer was the king (*Hioh*), surrounded by his guard. On his head he wore a net cap ("cawle") decorated with feathers in the same manner as the "crownes" described above, "but differing much both in fashion and perfectness of work." From the king's shoulders hung a waist-length coat of the skins of "conies." Members of his guard each wore a coat of similar cut, but of different skins. Some of the guard wore net caps "stuck with feathers," or covered with a light, downy substance, probably milkweed down. Only those persons who were close to the king wore the down-filled or down-covered net caps and feather plumes on their heads.

Following the procession of the king and his guard came the "naked sort of common people." Their long hair was gathered behind into a bunch in which were stuck plumes of feathers, but in the front were only single feathers which looked "like hornes." Every Indian had his face painted in black or white or other colors, and every man brought some sort of gift. The procession was brought up behind by the women and children. Each woman carried against her breast a round basket or so, filled with a number of articles such as bags of *Tobah*; a root called *Petah*, which was made into meal and either baked into bread or eaten raw; broiled pilchard-like fishes; and the seed and down of milkweed (?). The baskets are carefully described by Fletcher as "made in fashion like a deep boale . . . [and] about the brimmes they were hanged with peeces of shels of pearles, and in some places with two or three linkes at a place, of the chaines aforenamed: thereby signifying, that they were vessels wholly dedicated to the only vse of the gods they worshipped:

and besides this, they were wrought vpon with the matted downe of red feathers, distinguished into diuers workes and formes."

As the crowd of people came near, they gave a general salutation and were then silent. The scepter bearer, prompted by another man who whispered, delivered in a loud voice an oration which lasted half an hour. When the oration was ended, "there was a common *Amen*, in signe of approbation giuen by euery person . . ." Then the company, leaving the little children behind, came down to the foot of the hill where the English had their camp. Here the scepter bearer began to sing and danced in time to the song. The king, his guard, and all the others joined in the singing and dancing, except the women, who danced but did not sing. The women had torn faces, their bodies showed bruises and other lacerations which had been self-inflicted before the Indians had arrived. After the assembly of natives had concluded their dance, they indicated by signs that Drake should be seated. This done, the king and several others delivered orations to Drake, and, concluding with a song, placed the crown upon his head and hung all the shell disk bead necklaces around his neck. Many other gifts were tendered to Drake, and the name *Hioh* was bestowed upon him. Fletcher interpreted this ceremony as the giving up of the kingdom to Drake, a thought hardly ascribable to the Indians. It is quite clear, however, that Drake was individually and specially honored by the leader of the California natives, and was invested with a name, *Hioh*.

After the "crowning" was concluded, the common people, both men and women, dispersed among the English, "taking a diligent view and survey of every man." When a native found an Englishman who pleased his fancy, and the youthful Englishmen were preferred, a personal "sacrifice" in the form of weeping, moaning, shrieking, and tearing of the face with the fingernails was offered. As might be expected, such a scene was embarrassing and uncomfortable to the English, and the strongest efforts were of no avail in disabusing the Indians of their "idolatry." After a time the Indians quieted down and began to show to the English "their griefes and diseases which they carried about with them, some of them hauing old aches, some shruncke sinewes, some old soares and canckred vlcers, some wounds more lately receiued, and the like, in most lamentable manner crauing helpe and cure thereof from vs: making signes that if we did but blowe vpon their griefes, or but touched the diseased places, they would be whole." The English applied various unguents to the affected places, continuing the treatment as the natives resorted to the camp from time to time.

Now to analyze the happenings of June 26. The "Embassadors or messengers" of Fletcher are probably correctly identified, since the custom of having messengers who announce the coming of a chief and his party is known to have existed at least among the Pomo[69] and probably among the Coast Miwok, although there is no specific mention of such a practice among the latter. Even the custom that messengers should ask for a present for the "king" (i.e., chief) is known to have been observed by the Pomo.[70] It is impossible to identify the man who bore the "scepter" or "mace," a black stick about four and a half feet long, but the scepter itself seems identifiable with the staff known ethnographically to have been used in the central California Kuksu or ghost ceremony.[71]

The assemblage of the black stick with pendant "feathered crowns" and clamshell disk beads has not been noted by any modern ethnographer, but the flat, circular, centrally drilled white beads of clamshell are familiar (pl. 18, *c*). They were made from clamshells dug at Bodega Bay, the source of these beads for most of the Indians of central California.[72] It is of some interest to note that in later times the beads have been very abundant, and that in the last 350 years the manufacture and use of clamshell disk beads have been much increased. The net "crownes" covered with a pattern of colored feathers are described by Fletcher in terms so general that exact identification is difficult. They may have resembled some of those illustrated by Dixon, who collected them from the Northern Maidu.[73] At least, net caps with feather decorations were commonly used in Coast Miwok[74] and Pomo[75] ceremonies. The king's guard was probably composed of a number of male initiates of a secret society who naturally would separate themselves from the women and children when engaged in ceremonial duties.[76] The net cap of the king or *Hioh* was different from that of the others, and it is not improbable that it was one of the flicker-quill headbands so well known for the area (pl. 18, *a*).[77] This identification is at best tentative, however, since there was in this area a bewildering array of types of feather-decorated ceremonial headgear. The king's coat of conyskins seems to

---

[69] E. M. Loeb, *The Western Kuksu Cult*, Univ. Calif. Publ. Am. Arch. and Ethn., Vol. XXXIII, No. 1 (Berkeley, 1932), p. 49, and *Pomo Folkways*, p. 192; S. A. Barrett, *Ceremonies of the Pomo Indians*, Univ. Calif. Publ. Am. Arch. and Ethn., Vol. XII, No. 10 (Berkeley, 1917), p. 402, and "Pomo Buildings," p. 11.

[70] Barrett, *Ceremonies*, p. 403.

[71] Gifford and Kroeber, *Culture Element Distributions, IV: Pomo*, pp. 207–208; Loeb, *Pomo Folkways*, p. 366; Barrett, *Ceremonies*, p. 425. The Kuksu staff was feathered on the end, whereas that of Calnis was somewhat shorter and did not have the feather tuft. Kroeber, *Handbook*, pp. 261–262; Loeb, *The Western Kuksu Cult*, pp. 110, 128.

[72] They were manufactured chiefly by the Pomo and Northern Coast Miwok. See E. W. Gifford, *Clear Lake Pomo Society*, Univ. Calif. Publ. Am. Arch. and Ethn., Vol. XVIII, No. 2 (Berkeley, 1926), pp. 377–388; Kroeber, *Handbook*, p. 248; Kelly, "Coast Miwok Ethnography"; Gifford and Kroeber, *Culture Element Distributions, IV: Pomo*, (pp. 186–187).

[73] Dixon, "The Northern Maidu," figs. 29, 30, Pl. XLIX.

[74] Kelly, "Coast Miwok Ethnography."

[75] Barrett, *Ceremonies*, p. 433; Loeb, *Pomo Folkways*, p. 178.

[76] Cf. Barrett, *Ceremonies*, pp. 405, 438–439.

[77] Illustrated in Kroeber, *Handbook*, fig. 20. See also Gifford and Kroeber, elements 88, 89; Barrett, *Ceremonies*, p. 432; Kelly, "Coast Miwok Ethnography." And see Dixon, "The Northern Maidu," Pl. XLVIII, fig. 25.

have been distinguished from those of his guard. The guards' coats may have been made of pocket gopher or mountain beaver skins, and the king's coat was possibly of woven rabbitskin blankets, common to both the Pomo and the Coast Miwok.[78] What seems unusual is that there is no mention in Fletcher's account of the feather cloaks or skirts used in later times on ceremonial occasions. I have been unable to find any ethnographic data on a special skin coat for chiefs or ceremonial leaders. The down-filled head net undoubtedly refers to the central Californian net cap.[79] The feather plumes mentioned by Fletcher as worn on the head by persons close to the king may have been of several of the numerous types used in central California. Examples are illustrated by Dixon[80] and Kroeber.[81] The repeated mention by Fletcher of the use of feathers indicates clearly that their ceremonial use was highly developed at this period. The single feathers resembling "horns" are an ethnographic feature of the costume of the ghost dancer among the Pomo,[82] and although there is no documentary evidence that the Coast Miwok wore feathers in such a manner, it seems likely, in view of the very close correspondence between Pomo and Coast Miwok ceremonial features, that they did so. The practice of painting the body is an almost invariable feature of Coast Miwok[83] and Pomo[84] ceremonies.

The gifts brought by the women in round baskets included bags of *Tobah* (already discussed), broiled fish, the seed and down of some plant (milkweed?),[85] and a root called *Petah* or *Patah*. Neither the Pomo nor the Coast Miwok remember today any root or bulb with a name resembling *Petah* or *Patah*. Elmendorf and I have agreed with Kroeber that *Petah* is probably to be linked with the word "potato" in one or another of its various forms. Kroeber thinks that the description indicates the wild onion (*Brodiaea*), called *putcu* in Coast Miwok, and this is not improbable. However, soaproot (*Chlorogalum*), which was sometimes baked into a bread, would also fill the description. It is called *haka* by the Coast Miwok, and it is barely possible, though hardly probable, that *haka* could have been heard and recorded as *Patah* or *Petah*. Since

---

[78] Gifford and Kroeber, element no. 4. Kelly, "Coast Miwok Ethnography."

[79] Illustrated and described by Kroeber, *Handbook*, pl. 55, *a*, and pp. 264, 269, 388, and illustrated by Dixon, "The Northern Maidu," fig. 33. See also Gifford and Kroeber, elements nos. 81 ff.; Barrett, *Ceremonies*, pp. 407, 432; Loeb, *Pomo Folkways*, p. 200. The down-filled net cap was used by the Coast Miwok in the Kuksu and other ceremonial performances.

[80] Dixon, "The Northern Maidu," figs. 19–21.

[81] Kroeber, *Handbook*, fig. 21.

[82] Barrett, *Ceremonies*, p. 407, n. 12.

[83] Kelly, "Coast Miwok Ethnography"; Wagner, *Spanish Voyages*, pp. 158, 159 (Drake's Bay).

[84] Loeb, *Pomo Folkways*, p. 158; Barrett, *Ceremonies*, pp. 407, 433; Gifford and Kroeber, *Culture Element Distributions: IV, Pomo*. element no. 96, pp. 207–208.

[85] I can find no record that the down of milkweed (or of any other plant) was used. Most ethnographic accounts (see n. 79) above list the use of eagle down. That Fletcher was probably correct in attributing the source of the downy substance to a plant is shown by his reference tto the seeds of the same plant. There is also the probability that he saw the plant itself on the journey into the interior. From my own observation I know that at least three different plants producing such down grow on Point Reyes.

Fletcher speaks of *Petah* as a root, it seems improbable that he was describing acorns (called *ümba* in Coast Miwok); yet even this remote possibility may be entertained, since Madox recorded *cheepe* as bread, and Coast Miwok *tcipa* means acorn bread. The word *Petah*, and botanical identification, must remain in limbo until further data are at hand.

The feather-decorated baskets offer evidence, as Barrett and Kroeber have indicated, that Drake landed on the coast immediately north of San Francisco Bay. The baskets (pl. 19) are described as shaped like a deep bowl, covered with a matted down of red feathers worked into various patterns, and further embellished with pendant drops of pearl shell (*Haliotis*) and two or three disk beads in various places. Such baskets were made only by the Coast Miwok,[86] Pomo,[87] Lake Miwok, and Wappo. Kroeber states that these baskets "served as gifts and treasures; and above all they were destroyed in honor of the dead."[88] It is clear that, in 1579, feathered baskets similar in manufacture and use to the native baskets of today were known in this Coast Miwok area.

The scepter bearer, prompted in a low voice by another man, delivered a long oration. The Coast Miwok have such orators; among those Indians the office of speechmaker is a special one.[89] The Pomo have orators,[90] as do most other central Californians. The *Amen*, or sign of general approbation, following the oration has already been commented upon. Then the natives performed a dance to the accompaniment of a song led by the scepter bearer (or orator)[91] and joined in by the men, while the women danced but remained silent. Among the Pomo and Coast Miwok each ceremony has a song in connection with its observance.[92]

[86] Kelly, "Coast Miwok Ethnography." Dr. Kelly's informants at Bodega in describing just such baskets said, "They were just for show"—i.e., had no practical or utilitarian use. Her San Rafael informant also knew of such baskets.

[87] For illustrations and description see J. W. Hudson, "Pomo Basket Makers," *Overland Monthly*, ser. 2, XXI (1893), 571, and C. Purdy, "The Pomo Indian Baskets and Their Makers," *ibid.*, XV (1901), 438, 446. O. M. Dalton ("Notes on an Ethnographical Collection from the West Coast of North America . . . Formed during the Voyage of Captain Vancouver, 1790–1795," *Internationale Archiv für Ethnographie*, Vol. X [Leiden, 1897]), shows (fig. f, p. 232; Pl. XV, fig. 4) several Pomo baskets which might as well have been the ones described by Fletcher. It seems possible that these were collected at Bodega Bay, since some of the Vancouver party visited there, but this is not certain. In Mission times many Coast Miwok and even some Pomo were brought to San Francisco and San Jose as neophytes. These individuals might well account for the Pomo-Coast Miwok type of feathered baskets collected there in the early nineteenth century by von Langsdorff or Chamisso, both of whom illustrate such pieces in their published accounts. Barrett, *Pomo Indian Basketry*, Univ. Calif. Publ. Am. Arch. and Eth., Vol. VII, No. 3 (Berkeley, 1908), discusses at length (pp. 141–145, 168) feather and shell materials used in the manufacture of these decorated baskets. A number of examples are shown in Barrett's plate 21. The same anthropologist ("Pomo Buildings," pp. 1–17) mentions the use of feather-decorated baskets among the Pomo as sacrifices to the dead.

[88] Kroeber, *Handbook*, p. 245.

[89] Kelly, "Coast Miwok Ethnography."

[90] Gifford and Kroeber, *Culture Element Distributions, IV: Pomo*, element no. 807, p. 197, n.

[91] Barrett, *Ceremonies*, p. 400, mentions a principal singer who started and led the air of the songs, but does not indicate whether he might be identifiable with the "scepter bearer."

[92] See Barrett, *Ceremonies*, passim; Loeb, *The Western Kuksu Cult* and *Pomo Folkways*, passim; Kelly, "Coast Miwok Ethnography" *passim*.

The episode of the crowning has no parallel in native custom or ceremonial behavior, probably because "crowning" was a unique experience
for the Indians as well as the English. This fact should be kept in mind
in judging and estimating the native's actions and reactions—they were
as puzzled as the English. Drake was specifically honored by the Indians, and there is no reason to doubt Fletcher when he states that the
name *Hioh* was given to him. It has been suggested that *Hioh* was a
term of salutation or an interjection,[93] but there is no reason to believe
that this was so. The word finds possible equivalents in Coast Miwok
for chief, *hoipu*, *hoipa*, or friend, *oiya*.[94] Since the Interior Miwok word
for chief is *haiapo*, there is a bare possibility that the *hoi* of today may
have been rendered *hai* in 1579, though there is no direct evidence to
support this suggestion. It should be mentioned here that the Madox
account independently verifies Fletcher's remarks on the episode of the
crowning, as well as the word for "king" (chief?), which Madox renders
as *Hioghe*.[95]

The close scrutiny of the English by the Indians following the
"crowning" ceremony indicates that the main business of the day (i.e.,
the ceremonial crowning by secret society initiates) was over, and that
the general public could now take part in the festivities. Of great interest are Fletcher's statements to the effect that the most youthful Englishmen were repeatedly selected as recipients of personal sacrifice and
adoration which took the form of lamenting, moaning, weeping, wailing,
and self-lacerating. Only one conclusion can be drawn: the Indians supposed that they were looking upon relatives returned from the dead,
and hence performed the usual mourning observances.

After all these ceremonies were concluded, the Indians showed the
English their infirmities, aches, sores, and wounds, and it was made
clear that if the English would but blow upon them they would be made
well. This accords fairly well with the curing aspect of certain local
ceremonies. For example, the Kuksu doctor of the Pomo might cure by
blowing "his whistle over the various parts of his body, particularly
those recognized by the patients as the seats of pain."[96] There is no
mention of the use of whistles in connection with the ceremony enacted
by the Indians. Whistles are so commonly used in local ceremonies that
their omission is noteworthy. The detailed nature of the account indi-

---

[93] Wagner, *Drake's Voyage*, p. 492, n. 37. Wagner says that this word "sounds" to him like an excla-
mation. To Elmendorf and me it "sounds" like the Coast Miwok word for chief or friend.The latter
proposal rests upon both phonetic and semantic resemblances.

[94] For the Coast Miwok words for "chief" and "friend" see Barrett, *The Ethno-Geography of the
Pomo Indians*, words nos. 62, 64, pp. 70, 71. The Pomo words (p. 58) are totally unlike those of
the Coast Miwok. Barrett, *Ceremonies*, mentions a Kuksu curing call, *hyo*, which was repeated
four times. Although the call is phonetically similar, the context is so unlike, that a correspondence
with Fletcher's word for chief or king is improbable.

[95] Taylor, *loc. cit.*, p. 369.

[96] Barrett, *Ceremonies*, pp. 412, 431; Loeb, *The Western Kuksu Cult*, p. 118.

cates that this feature was not so strongly developed in 1579 as it is today in local native custom.

General observations, and occurrences from June 27 to July 23.—The natives were almost constant visitors, and it is noted that ordinarily every third day they brought their "sacrifices" (?). From this and other indications it seems possible that the ceremonial number of the Indians was three. The ceremonial number of the adjoining Pomo is four.[97] The Coast Miwok ceremonial number was probably four, though there is no direct evidence to support this supposition. The Indian bow is spoken of as weak and "more fit for children than for men," a remark to be expected from the English, who were even then employing the famous longbow. The English were impressed with the strength of the natives, but, for Indians accustomed to transporting everything on their backs, their feats of strength seem not surprising. It is also noted that the natives were good at running and that this was the ordinary means of travel. The English admired the native surf fishing. Kroeber has interpreted the passage, "if at any time, they chanced to see a fish, so neere the shoare, that they might reach the place without swimming, they would neuer, or very seldome misse to take it," as signifying diving for fish in the surf. Since this unusual practice is not otherwise recorded ethnographically for any coastal Californian tribe, some other explanation may be in order, and I suggest that Fletcher may have had reference to surf fishing with a round hand net, a practice known to have been followed by the Coast Miwok.[98] One gets the impression that the English found much to admire in their native friends.

Drake, his gentlemen, and others of the ship's company made an expedition into the interior to see the native villages and the country round about. The houses were all of the semisubterranean, circular type discussed previously. Two animals were seen, as also herds of deer and great numbers of "conies," a name which, as used by Fletcher, seems to fit no known animal living today in this coastal area.[99]

The country was named *Albion* "in respect of the white bancks and cliffes, which lie toward the sea . . . ," and a post was set up with an engraved brass plate nailed to it. The white cliffs are one of the most conspicuous features of Drake's Bay.[100] That the plate of brass has been found at Drake's Bay is a fact of the greatest significance.

Upon the departure of the English, the Indians were sorrowful, and they burned a "sacrifice" of a string of disk beads and a bunch of feathers. The burning of shell beads in memory and honor of the dead,

[97] Kroeber, *Handbook*, table 10, p. 876.
[98] Kelly, "Coast Miwok Ethnography."
[99] The ground squirrel and Point Reyes mountain beaver have been variously identified as Fletcher's "conies." See Wagner, *Drake's Voyage*, p. 492–493, n. 42.
[100] See photograph in McAdie, "Nova Albion—1579," fig. 1.

a custom which Fletcher may have described, is known for the Coast Miwok,[101], Pomo,[102] and neighboring groups.[103]

Aside from those actions of the natives which are usually associated with their attitudes toward the dead (weeping, moaning, self-laceration, use of feathered baskets, sacrifice of shell beads and feathers in the fire), there are other evidences that the English were regarded as the returned spirits of the dead. First is Fletcher's observation that the Indians were "standing when they drew neere, as men rauished in their mindes, with the sight of such things as they neuer had seene, or heard of before that time: their errand being rather with submission and feare to worship vs as Gods, then to haue any warre with vs as with mortall men. Which thing as it did partly shew it selfe at that instant, so did it more and more manifest it selfe afterwards, during the whole time of our abode amongst them." Except for the sole occasion, at the conclusion of the ceremony on June 26, when the Indians embraced the youthful Englishmen, the natives seem to have avoided touching the whites. This is most understandable if it is believed that they looked upon the English as the dead returned,[104] for bodily contact with a dead person or spirit was certain, in their minds, to have disastrous results. Further evidence of this may be contained in the statement: "Our General hauing now bestowed vpon them diuers things, at their departure they restored them all againe; none carrying with him any thing of whatsoeuer hee had receiued . . ." There is one more bit of inferential evidence along this line which comes from the Madox account. This is the phrase *Nocharo mu*, "touch me not" (i.e., *notcáto mu*, "keep away"). It may be asked why Madox recorded this particular phrase out of the many his informant must have heard. The answer is perhaps to be found in the simple fact that the English heard this phrase uttered a great many times, and it stuck in their memory. In view of the fact that the natives held the English in fear as dead people, the phrase "touch me not" might often have been used toward amorous sailors, or against any form of bodily contact.

ADDITIONAL ETHNOGRAPHIC ITEMS IN THE RICHARD MADOX AND JOHN DRAKE ACCOUNTS

In the second deposition of John Drake, cousin to Francis Drake (see below, App. I), there is no new information. There is, however, independent corroboration of the weeping and self-laceration referred to

---

[101] Kelly, "Coast Miwok Ethnography."
[102] Kroeber, *Handbook*, p. 277.
[103] These "burnt offerings" are ascribed to the Trinidad Bay Yurok by Wagner (*Drake's Voyage*, p. 157), but there is no need to look so far afield for parallels when the Coast Miwok–Pomo area fits the case so well.
[104] Memorial ceremonies for the dead are a characteristic feature of central California culture; see Loeb, *The Western Kuksu Cu*, p. 117 (Coast Miwok).

repeatedly in the *World Encompassed* account. The natives are mentioned as having bows and arrows and as being naked, both of which items are mentioned by Fletcher. The Indians' sadness at the departure of the English, as remarked by John Drake, is a further verification of Fletcher's observations as presented in some detail in *The World Encompassed*.

The brief Madox account is of particular interest since a number of words in the Indian language, a song, and the episode of the crowning are mentioned. The linguistic items are given as follows:

Cheepe	bread	*Nocharo mu*	tuch me not
Huchee kecharoh	sit downe	*Hioghe*	a king

As Elmendorf and I have already pointed out, the vocabulary may be assigned conclusively to the Coast Miwok language.[105] *Cheepe*, "bread," is equivalent to modern Coast Miwok *tcipa*, "acorn bread." This word alone is the clearest possible evidence that Drake's Indian acquaintances were Coast Miwok. *Huchee kecharoh*, "sit down," probably is an incorrect translation of the phrase. The closest approximation in modern Coast Miwok is *atci kotcáto*, "step into the house," and *hoki kotcádo*, "go into the house" (*tc* is phonetically equivalent to the sound *ch* as in chin). It is possible to explain these differently stated meanings of these phonetically similar phrases as owing to incorrect inductions of meaning under specific circumstances. Kelly's Coast Miwok ethnographic informants stated that, according to old custom, whenever people came to a house they were asked to walk in and were offered a seat in the rear of the house, and food was placed before them. In some such situation, particularly if the English had occasion to be often in the Indian village, they may have repeatedly heard the invitation, "step into the house." Likewise, the phrase *Nocharo mu*, "touch me not," may have been translated by Madox (or his informant) only vaguely, since it represents a situation rather than a concrete object, which would be less liable to misinterpretation. Modern Coast Miwok offers a close parallel in the form of *notcáto mu*, which may be literally translated "stay over there," or "stay away" (*notca*, "farther," "yonder").

Madox's word for king, *Hioghe*, is similar to that given by Fletcher (*Hioh* or *Hyoh*), except that the *ghe* ending is unusual. From the words of the Indian song given by Madox (see below), in which *heigh* (i.e., *hai*) appears, it might be suspected that the *gh* is silent; yet why is the terminal *e* present? It may be that if *Hioghe* were exactly similar phonetically to *Hioh*, there would not be a terminal *e* in *Hioghe*. Thus Madox's *Hioghe* may indicate a terminal sound (short or weak *e*?) and therefore be close to modern Coast Miwok *hoipa* (and Sierra Miwok *haiapo*).

---

[105] Heizer and Elmendorf, "Francis Drake's California Anchorage."

That the *gh* might be an indication of the *p* sound is possible, or, again, it could represent Madox's attempt to render a weak or indefinite labial sound which was imperfectly remembered by his informant. Too close a phonetic transcription of an Indian language by Elizabethan Englishmen should not be expected—there was little standardization in English spelling[106] at that time. The foregoing is not advanced as an argument to show that the terminal "e" was sounded, but is merely presented as a possibility. Elizabethan English commonly used an unpronounced terminal "e." The song of the Indians "when they worship god" is given by Madox as *Hodeli oh heigh oh heigh ho hodali oh*. No Coast Miwok or Pomo song on record accords exactly with that given by Madox, although some are quite similar. For example, a Coast Miwok *Suya* song transcribed by Kelly is a repetitive line *Yo ya he yo he o*. Other examples from the Coast Miwok are not available, but some Pomo ceremonial songs may be cited. Stephen Powers[107] gives a Sanel Pomo song:

> *Hel-lel-li-ley*
> *Hel-lel-lo*
> *Hel-lel-lu*

E. M. Loeb[108] gives several Pomo songs which are associated with the Kuksu or ghost ceremony:

> 1. *He yo he yo he yo*
>   *He yoha eheya ye*
>   *To ya he yo ho ho*
> 2. *Tali, tali, yo yo weya yo, weya yo, ha hi he ya he hotsaii ya hi ho.*
> 3. *He ha le me, le lu hi ma humane, hu ...*

Other Pomo songs used in ceremonies are given by Loeb:[109]

> 1. *Ū ū hulai leli ha ha.*
> 2. *He he la le ha hi hi hi, ya ya ya, hu wa!*
> 3. *Yo yo hale e he na gagoyá ō he he!*
> 4. *Ho yu ko, he he, a ha a a. Hi ye ko, lai ye ko, He tsi ye.*
> 5. *Yo ho yo ho yaho, he yo ho waha.*

These examples show how generally similar are the Coast Miwok[110] and Pomo ceremonial songs of today to the song of 1579 given by

---

[106] For evidence of this, using the words on Drake's plate of brass, see Allen Chickering, "Some Notes with Regard to Drake's Plate of Brass" and "Further Notes on the Drake Plate."

[107] Powers, *Tribes of California*, p. 171. Cf. the Huchnom song facing p. 144.

[108] Loeb, *The Western Kuksu Cult*, pp. 103, 127, 128.

[109] Loeb, *Pomo Folkways*, pp. 374, 392, 393. See also Barrett, *Ceremonies*, pp. 409, 413.

[110] Because of the high degree of similarity between all phases of Pomo and Coast Miwok ceremonies, a close correspondence, or even identity, in the songs connected with these ceremonies may safely be assumed.

Madox. Here again an exact correspondence should not be expected, since it is not known whether the song given by Madox was one associated with a particular ceremonial occurrence, nor is it known how changeable these songs are. And again, in the time that has passed and in the changing course of circumstances since 1579, some exactness has almost inevitably been sacrificed. Madox's statement that the natives sang "one dauncing first wh his handes up, and al ye rest after lyke ye prest and people" verifies Fletcher's description of the singing and dancing at the time of the great ceremony of June 26.

Supposed Indian Traditions of Drake's Visit

Professor George Davidson was the second investigator to use an Indian tradition as evidence of the Drake's Bay location of the 1579 visit.[111] The source of the tradition is in J. P. Munro-Fraser's *History of Marin County*,[112] and is stated as follows:

First of all comes an old Indian legend which comes down through the Nicasios to the effect that Drake did land at this place [Drake's Bay]. Although they have been an interior tribe ever since the occupation by the Spaniards and doubtless were at that time, it still stands to reason that they would know all about the matter. If the ship remained in the bay thirty-six days it is reasonable to suppose that a knowledge of its presence reached every tribe within an area of one hundred miles and that the major portion of them paid a visit to the bay to see the "envoys of the Great Spirit," as they regarded the white seamen. One of these Indians named Theognis who is reputed to have been one hundred and thirty years old when he made the statement, says that Drake presented the Indians with a dog, some young pigs, and seeds of several species of grain . . . The Indians also state that some of Drake's men deserted him here, and, making their way into the country, became amalgamated with the aboriginals to such an extent that all traces of them were lost, except possibly a few names [Nicasio, Novato] which are to be found among the Indians.

Wagner feels that there is no reason or evidence to indicate that the Nicasio Indian tradition refers to Drake,[113] a conclusion with which I agree. If any early expedition did leave pigs with the Coast Miwok, it could have been the Spanish one of 1793, which attempted unsuccessfully to form a settlement at Bodega Bay. Felipe Goycoechea, in 1793 specifically mentions seeing some pigs and chickens which the Spanish had left earlier in the year with the Indians at that place.[114] With Wagner's statement that, if any credit can be given to the pig episode, Cermeño may have been the donor,[115] I cannot agree, mainly for the reason that Cermeño's crew were hungry and would not have given the

[111] Davidson, "Identification of Sir Francis Drake's Anchorage," p. 35.
[112] J. P. Munro-Fraser, *History of Marin County* (San Francisco, 1880), pp. 96–97.
[113] Wagner, *Drake's Voyage*, pp. 148, 167, 494.
[114] Wagner, "The Last Spanish Exploration," p. 334.
[115] Wagner, *Drake's Voyage*, p. 167.

Indians any pigs if they had had them. The story of the dog is interesting since neither the Pomo nor Coast Miwok had dogs in pre-Spanish times, and the evidence indicates that dogs were introduced shortly after 1800.[116] Aside from these facts, the supposed Nicasio tradition does not have a true ring—it is not the type of story that Indians are accustomed to tell.

A belief among the Coast Miwok[117] and some Pomo[118] tribes that the home of the dead is associated with Point Reyes should perhaps be taken into account. The belief is that this seaward projection is associated with the dead, who follow a string leading out through the surf to the land of the dead. It is barely possible that this belief, which is quite clearly of Coast Miwok origin, is a legendary reminiscence of Drake's visit which seems to have been, in part at least, interpreted by the Indians as the return of the dead. It may be superfluous to mention that no Indian has ever stated his idea of the origin of this legend,[119] or of its association with the visit of Drake's party; yet there remains the possibility that the occurrence made an impression so deep that Point Reyes became in this way associated with the home of the dead in the west, from which the English were supposed to have come and gone. If this tradition were associated with Drake, it would, of course, signify that his anchorage was behind Point Reyes in Drake's Bay. On the other hand, this remarkable point which juts far out into the ocean is a prominent feature of Coast Miwok territory, and by reason of its unique topography might have been associated with local ceremonial beliefs.[120]

I may conclude this discussion by saying that no direct evidence of Drake's visit in 1579 is to be found in recorded local Indian traditions. In view of the long time that has intervened, no native legendary evidence is to be expected. Euhemerism is ordinarily rather an unproductive and hazardous approach for the historian.

RECAPITULATION AND CONCLUSION

The results of this survey can now be weighed and a solution to the problem of the location of Drake's California anchorage suggested.

It has been shown that there is not a scrap of ethnographic evidence to suggest that Drake landed in Trinidad Bay and saw the Yurok Indians. The Hondius *Portus Novae Albionis* might apply equally to

[116] A. L. Kroeber, *Culture Element Distributions, XV: Salt, Dogs, Tobacco,* Univ. Calif. Anthro. Rec., Vol. VI, No. 1 (Berkeley, 1941), pp. 6 ff., map 5.
[117] Kelly, "Coast Miwok Ethnography."
[118] Powers, *Tribes of California,* p. 200.
[119] Kelly's informant did say that "before steamers used to travel along the coast" certain occurrences in connection with this belief in the land of the dead took place. This may be a memory of an incident which once was more specifically remembered. At best, however, it is improbable that there would be any tradition of Drake's visit per se.
[120] Such incidents are not uncommon in California. Note, for example, the legendary significance of Mount Diablo to the Indian tribes of central California.

Bodega Bay or Drake's Bay, and by itself can only rise to the level of supporting, rather than primary, evidence. Thus, in reference to the Trinidad Bay theory, the map cannot alone and unaided prove the point against the overwhelming evidence to the contrary.

The ethnographic evidence indicates strongly, indeed almost conclusively, that Drake landed in territory occupied by Coast Miwok Indians.[121] Since Pomo culture and Coast Miwok Indian culture were so similar as to be almost indistinguishable, the culture described by Fletcher might refer to either Coast Miwok or Pomo, and no solution would be forthcoming were it not for the additional fact that *all* the unquestionably native words (*Hioh, Gnaah, Huchee kecharo, Nocharo mu, Cheepe*) are of Coast Miwok derivation. It may therefore be concluded that Drake had contact mainly with the Coast Miwok. Any effort to prove that the customs described point expressly to the Pomo as Drake's visitors would have to deny the linguistic proofs and rest upon the unlikely assumption that Pomo and Coast Miwok culture were markedly divergent in 1579.[122] The Pomo ethnographic data cited here are therefore to be looked upon not as unique Pomo cultural traits, but as supplementary, comparative material which is at a premium for the Coast Miwok. But there are two bays in Coast Miwok territory to which Drake might have brought his ship. These are Drake's Bay and Bodega Bay.

No internal evidence points specifically to either Drake's or Bodega Bay—the accounts lack geographical detail,[123] the ethnographic Coast Miwok culture was in operation in both bays, and contemporary maps are so inaccurate and open to variable interpretation that nothing definite can be ascertained from their inspection. What is needed, therefore, is some hint or lead which will break this stalemate. There are two such leads. The first is the plate of brass left by Drake and recently found at Drake's Bay. Granted the authenticity of the Drake plate, it now does not rank as an isolated find, however spectacular, but rather as good

---

[121] I disagree with Wagner's statement (*Drake's Voyage*, p. 169): "The truth probably is that Drake stopped at two or three different places on the coast [Trinidad Bay, Bodega Bay] and the writer of the original narrative or the compilers who worked on it embodied in one description those of all the Indians he met." The part of the *World Encompassed* account treated here has shown itself to be a homogeneous description, interspersed with some naïve interpretation of west-central California coast Indian culture, and cannot be looked upon as a composite description. To believe otherwise would seriously distort the facts. This conclusion I submit as one of the most important results of the present inquiry.

[122] Wagner, *Drake's Voyage*, pp. 492–495, does select the Pomo as having the customs and manners described by Fletcher. In this he was inevitably guided by the more abundant Pomo data. Kroeber's selection of Drake's Bay as the site of the anchorage (*Handbook*, p. 278) rests upon the same grounds as my conclusion. Wagner (*Drake's Voyage*, p. 497, n. 10) takes issue with Kroeber and raises several objections without answering them satisfactorily.

[123] Wagner is concerned over this fact. He says (*Drake's Voyage*, p. 498, n. 24) that a reference to Drake's Estero should have been included in the narrative "since the Indian villages were almost entirely located upon it." In answer it may be observed that the Indian villages of Drake's time were situated sporadically around the shore of Drake's Bay as well as on the estero. One might as well ask at the same time why Fletcher did not mention Tomales Bay if Drake were at Bodega?

supporting evidence of the conclusion based upon my ethnographic analysis. The second point of evidence is Fletcher's statement that "this country our generall named *Albion*, and that for two causes; the one in respect of the white bancks and cliffes, which lie toward the sea: the other, that it might have some affinity, euen in name also, with our owne country, which was sometime so called." The *Famous Voyage* version says almost the same, except that the country was named *Nova Albion*, which agrees more closely with the wording of the Drake plate. Wagner has discussed the white cliffs,[124] but his argument is unconvincing. There is no good reason to doubt that the cliffs mentioned were at the bay, since Fletcher implies that the naming took place before the departure.[125] And it must be remembered that white cliffs which face toward the sea[126] are at Drake's Bay and *not at Bodega*.

In June, 1579, then, Drake probably landed in what is now known as Drake's Bay. He remained there for five weeks repairing his ship, and found the Indians the most remarkable objects of interest with which he came in contact. From a comparative analysis of the detailed descriptions of the native ceremonies, artifacts, and language I conclude that in the fullest authentic account, *The World Encompassed*, it is the Coast Miwok Indians that are referred to.

---

[124] Wagner, *Drake's Voyage*, p. 151.

[125] And, significantly, the Drake plate of brass uses the words "Nova Albion." This is independently attested by John Drake in his first declaration.

[126] See Francisco de Bolaños' explicit mention of the white cliffs in Drake's Bay as prominent landmarks (Wagner, *Drake's Voyage*, p. 498, n. 19). See also Davidson, "Identification of Sir Francis Drake's Anchorage," p. 31. Richard Madox refers to the California anchorage as "Ships Land," perhaps the name given to the place by the sailors themselves.

Appendix I

THE SOURCES

THERE ARE in existence at least three useful independent accounts of Sir Francis Drake's California visit in 1579. These are: (1) the *World Encompassed* and the similar *Famous Voyage* accounts; (2) the second deposition of John Drake, and (3) the valuable notes of Richard Madox.

The Famous Voyage and The World Encompassed.—The *Famous Voyage*, first printed in 1589, was compiled by Richard Hakluyt from three sources—John Cooke's manuscript, the *Anonymous Narrative*, and the Francis Fletcher manuscript.[1] *The World Encompassed*, which probably was in manuscript form a few years after Drake's return to England, did not appear in print until 1628. The sources of this account are the Fletcher manuscript, the Edward Cliffe account, and the relations of Nuño da Silva and López de Vaz.[2] It is obvious to any reader that the *Famous Voyage* and *World Encompassed* accounts of the California Indians are closely similar in wording, the chief difference between the two being that the latter account is fuller than the former.[3] The richer detail does not indicate literary padding, since the additional information is ethnographically sound. One gets the impression that the *Famous Voyage* version is an abridgement of *The World Encompassed* account itself, or perhaps its source, though if this is so in fact only the bibliographers can tell. Henry R. Wagner has carefully analyzed the various accounts of the Drake voyage,[4] and is inclined, no doubt with good reason, to treat the *World Encompassed* version as "untrustworthy"; yet this characterization hardly holds for what it tells of the California Indians, which, within limits of interpretation, is a straightforward, detailed ethnographic record, of convincing authenticity.

It is fairly certain that Francis Fletcher's "Notes" was the source of the description of California Indian manners and customs, since, as Wagner points out, the descriptions of the Patagonians and Fuegians in the first half of the Fletcher manuscript (the second half is now lost) agree very closely in wording with the descriptions of the California coast Indians.[5]

Of Francis Fletcher, chaplain and diarist of the Drake expedition, O. M. Dalton says:

---

[1] Henry R. Wagner, *Sir Francis Drake's Voyage around the World* (San Francisco, 1926), p. 241.
[2] *Ibid.*, pp. 287, 289.
[3] *The World Encompassed* account of Drake in California is reprinted in Appendix II, below. It is printed in full in Volume XVI of the Hakluyt Society publications (ed. W. S. Vaux; London, 1854). The *Famous Voyage* is easily accessible in *Drake's Plate of Brass*, California Historical Society, Special Publication No. 13 (San Francisco, 1937), pp. 27–30.
[4] Wagner, *Drake's Voyage*, pp. 229 ff., n. 1.
[5] *Ibid.*, pp. 61, 147, 245, 290.

. . . it may . . . be suggested that Fletcher was not such a romancer as has sometimes been supposed. There is really a large amount of information condensed in his few pages,—as much, or perhaps more, than is to be found in many chapters of later and more diffuse historians or travellers. That he should have seen strange and unprecedented occurrences in the light of his own limited knowledge and of the narrow experience of his time, was after all a psychological necessity. His narrative, like the sea-god Glaucus in Plato's Republic, is obscured by strange incrustations; nevertheless with a little patience the fictitious shell may be removed and the solid fact discovered intact beneath it . . . It is apparent that the whole passage describing Drake's interview with the "King," on which some ridicule has been cast, is chiefly absurd because the narrator inevitably reads into the social conditions of an uncultured tribe something of the European etiquette of the day . . . It was only natural that a difficulty should have been experienced by minds, not scientifically trained, in finding an appropriate terminology by which to describe unfamiliar objects . . . Other instances might be quoted, but the above are sufficient to show that Fletcher described scenes that actually passed before his eyes, while the inferences he drew from them were erroneous. It is only fair, if small things may be compared with great, that the humble chronicler of a later day should be accorded the same liberal method of interpretation which has long been granted to classical authors.[6]

John Drake's Second Declaration.—John Drake was the orphan son of Robert Drake, who was the uncle of Francis Drake. John Drake accompanied his cousin on the voyage round the world, and subsequently went along on the Edward Fenton expedition, was shipwrecked in the River Plate (1582), taken captive by the Indians, and escaped only to fall into the hands of the Spanish. John Drake was questioned by the authorities, and in his second deposition there is a brief account of the occurrences in California, 1579.[7]

There he [Francis Drake] landed and built huts and remained a month and a half, caulking his vessel. The victuals they found were mussels and sea-lions. During that time many Indians came there and when they saw the Englishmen they wept and scratched their faces with their nails until they drew blood, as though this were an act of homage or adoration. By signs Captain Francis told them not to do that, for the Englishmen were not God. These people were peaceful and did no harm to the English, but gave them no food. They are of the colour of the Indians here [Peru] and are comely. They carry bows and arrows and go naked. The climate is temperate, more cold than hot. To all appearance it is a very good country. Here he caulked his large ship and left

[6] O. M. Dalton, "Notes on an Ethnographical Collection . . . Formed during the Voyage of Captain Vancouver, 1790–1795," *Internationale Archiv für Ethnographie*, Vol. X (Leiden, 1897), p. 235. A. L. Kroeber says, "The passage is a somewhat prolix mixture of narration and depiction . . ." (*Handbook of the Indians of California*, Bureau of American Ethnology, Bull. 78 [Washington, D. C., 1925], pp. 275–276).

[7] For details see Zelia Nuttall, *New Light on Drake*, Hakluyt Society, ser. 2, Vol. 34 (London, 1914), pp. 18–23. See also Wagner, *Drake's Voyage*, pp. 328–334.

the ship he had taken in Nicaragua. He departed, leaving the Indians, to all appearances, sad.[8]

Richard Madox's Account of California.—In 1932, Miss E. G. R. Taylor discovered in the diary of Richard Madox, Chaplain aboard Edward Fenton's ship in 1582, some remarks on Drake's visit on the California coast in 1579.[9] Madox was not a member of the Drake expedition, and it is safe to assume that his notes consist of information received in conversation with some of Fenton's crew who had accompanied Drake. These could have been William Hawkins, John Drake, Thomas Hood, and Thomas Blackcollar.[10] Miss Taylor notes Madox's categorical statement that "Syr Frances Drake graved and bremd his ship at 48 degrees to ye north" together with evidence from other sources, and concludes that "it would appear that Drake's anchorage must be sought in Oregon rather than in California, perhaps in Gray's Bay, or at the mouth of the Raft River." Miss Taylor had hoped to get a clue from the Madox vocabulary, but was unsuccessful. Henry Wagner has answered Miss Taylor's Oregon claim effectively,[11] and the identification of the Madox vocabulary as Coast Miwok is further proof that the statement "at 48 degrees" is an error. The log raft depicted by Madox and discussed by Miss Taylor and Mr. Wagner is a typical Peruvian sailing raft, as reference to S. K. Lothrop's detailed paper will demonstrate;[12] it has no relation whatsoever to California.

The relevant portion of Madox's account is as follows:

In ships land wh is ye back syde of Labradore and as Mr. Haul [Christopher Hall] supposeth nye thereunto Syr Frances Drake graved and bremd his ship at 48 degrees to ye north. Ye people ar for feature color apparel diet and holo speach lyke to those of Labradore and is thowght kyngles for they crowned Syr Frances Drake. Ther language is thus.

   Cheepe   bread
   Huchee kecharoh   sit downe
   Nocharo mu   tuch me not
   Hioghe   a king

Ther song when they worship god is thus—one dauncing first wh his handes up, and al ye rest after lyke ye prest and people *Hodeli oh heigh oh heigh ho hodali oh*

Yt is thowght yt they of Labradore [do] worship ye son and ye moon but [whether they] do of calphurnia I kno not. . . .[13]

---

[8] Nuttall, *New Light on Drake*, pp. 50–51.
[9] For details see E. G. R. Taylor, "Francis Drake and the Pacific: Two Fragments," *Pacific Historical Review*, I (1932), 360–369.
[10] For details see *ibid.*, pp. 363–365; Henry R. Wagner, "George Davidson, Geographer of the Northwest Coast," *California Historical Society Quarterly*, XI (1932), 309–311; and Nuttall, *New Light on Drake*, pp. 19–20.
[11] Wagner, "George Davidson," pp. 310–311.
[12] S. K. Lothrop, "Aboriginal Navigation off the West Coast of South America," *Journal of the Royal Anthropological Institute*, LXII (1932), 235–238, figs. 9*a*, 9*b*, 10.
[13] Reprinted from Taylor, *loc. cit.*, p. 369.

EXTRACT FROM "THE WORLD ENCOMPASSED BY SIR FRANCIS DRAKE"

London: Printed for Nicholas Bovrne, 1628. "Carefully collected out of the Notes of Master Francis Fletcher *Preacher in this employment, and diuers others his followers in the same.*" (Pp. 64–81.)[1]

In 38 deg. 30 min. we fell with a conuenient and fit harborough, and Iune 17. came to anchor therein: where we continued till the 23. day of Iuly following. During all which time, notwithstanding it was in the height of Summer, and so neere the Sunne; yet were wee continually visited with like nipping colds, as we had felt before; insomuch that if violent exercises of our bodies, and busie imployment about our necessarie labours, had not sometimes compeld vs to the contrary, we could very well haue beene contented to haue kept about vs still our Winter clothes; yea (had not necessities suffered vs) to haue kept our beds; neither could we at any time in whole fourteene dayes together, find the aire so cleare as to be able to take the height of Sunne or starre. . . . [Omitted here is a lengthy discourse on the weather.]

The next day after our comming to anchor in the aforesaid harbour, the people of the countrey shewed themselues; sending off a man with great expedition to vs in a canow. Who being yet but a little from the shoare, and a great way from our ship, spake to vs continually as he came rowing on. And at last at a reasonable distance staying himselfe, he began more solemnely a long and tedious oration, after his manner: vsing in the deliuerie thereof, many gestures and signes, mouing his hands, turning his head and body many wayes; and after his oration ended, with great shew of reuerence and submission, returned back to shoare againe. He shortly came againe the second time in like manner, and so the third time: When he brought with him (as a present from the rest) a bunch of feathers, much like the feathers of a blacke crow, very neatly and artificially gathered vpon a string, and drawne together into a round bundle; being verie cleane and finely cut, and bearing in length an equall proportion one with another; a speciall cognizance (as wee afterwards obserued) which they that guard their kings person, weare on their heads. With this also he brought a little basket made of rushes, and filled with an herb which they called *Tabah.* Both which being tyed to a short rodde, he cast into our boate. Our Generall intended to haue recompenced him immediately with many good things, he would haue bestowed vpon him: but entring into the boate to deliuer the same, he could not be drawne to receiue them by any means: saue one hat, which being cast into the water out of the ship, he tooke vp (refusing vtterly to meddle with any other thing, though it were vpon a board put off vnto him) and so presently made his returne. After which time, our boate could row no way, but wondring at vs as at gods, they would follow the same with admiration.

The 3. day following, viz. the 21. our ship hauing receiued a leake at sea, was brought to anchor neerer the shoare, that her goods being landed, she might be repaired: but for that we were to preuent any danger, that might chance

---

[1] As printed in *Drake's Plate of Brass*, California Historical Society, Special Publication No. 13 (San Francisco, 1937). pp. 32–46.

against our safety, our generall first of all landed his men, with all necessary prouision, to build tents and make a fort for the defence of our selues and goods: and that wee might vnder the shelter of it, with more safety (what euer should befall) end our businesse; which when the people of the country perceiued vs doing, as men set on fire to war, in defence of their countrie, in great hast and companies, with such weapons as they had, they came downe vnto vs; and yet with no hostile meaning, or intent to hurt vs: standing when they drew neare, as men rauished in their mindes, with the sight of such things as they neuer had seene, or heard of before that time: their errand being rather with submission and feare to worship vs as Gods, then to haue any warre with vs as with mortall men. Which thing is it did partly shew it selfe at that instant, so did it more and more manifest it selfe afterwards, during the whole time of our abode amongst them. At this time, being willed by signes to lay from them their bowes and arrowes, they did as they were directed, and so did all the rest, as they came more and more by companies vnto them, growing in a little while, to a great number both of men and women.

To the intent therefore, that this peace which they themselues so willingly sought, might without any cause of breach thereof, on our part giuen, be continued; and that wee might with more safety and expedition, end our businesses in quiet; our Generall with all his company, vsed all meanes possible, gently to intreate them, bestowing vpon each of them liberally, good and necessary things to couer their nakednesse, withall signifying vnto them, we were no Gods but men, and had neede of such things to couer our owne shame; teaching them to vse them to the same ends: for which cause also wee did eate and drinke in their presence, giuing them to vnderstand, that without that wee could not liue, and therefore were but men as well as they.

Notwithstanding nothing could perswade them, nor remoue that opinion, which they had conceiued of vs, that wee should be Gods.

In recompence of those things which they had receiued of vs, as shirts linnen cloth, &c. they betsowed vpon our generall, and diuerse of our company, diuerse things, as feathers, cawles of networke, the quiuers of their arrowes, made of fawne-skins, and the very skins of beasts that their women wore vpon their bodies. Hauing thus had their fill of this times visiting and beholding of vs, they departed with ioy to their houses, which houses are digged round within the earth, and haue from the vppermost brimmes of the circle, clefts of wood set vp, and ioyned close together at the top, like our spires on the steeple of a church: which being couered with earth, suffer no water to enter, and are very warme, the doore in the most part of them, performes the office of a chimney, to let out the smoake: its made in bignesse and fashion, like to an ordinary scuttle in a ship, and standing slopewise: their beds are the hard ground, onely with rushes strewed vpon it, and lying round about the house, haue their fire in the middest, which by reason that the house is but low vaulted, round and close, giueth a maruelous reflexion to their bodies to heate the same.

Their men for the most part goe naked, the women take a kinde of bulrushes, and kembing it after the manner of hempe, make themselues thereof a loose garment, which being knitte about their middles, hanges downe about their hippes, and so affordes to them a couering of that, which nature teaches should be hidden: about their shoulders, they weare also the skin of a deere, with the haire vpon it. They are very obedient to their husbands, and exceeding ready in all seruices: yet of themselues offring to do nothing, without the consents, or being called of the men.

As soone as they were returned to their houses, they began amongst themselues a kind of most lamentable weeping & crying out; which they continued also a great while together, in such sort, that in the place where they left vs (being neere about 3-quarters of an English mile distant from them) we very plainely, with wonder and admiration did heare the same; the women especially, extending their voices, in a most miserable and dolefull manner of shreeking.

Notwithstanding this humble manner of presenting themselues, and awfull demeanour vsed towards vs, we thought it no wisedome too farre to trust them (our experience of former Infidels dealing with vs before, made vs carefull to prouide against an alteration of their affections, or breach of peace if it should happen) and therefore with all expedition we set vp our tents, and entrenched ourselues with walls of stone: that so being fortified within ourselues, we might be able to keepe off the enemie (if they should so proue) from comming amongst vs without our good wills: this being quickly finished we went the more cheerefully and securely afterward, about our other businesse.

Against the end of two daies (during which time they had not againe beene with vs) there was gathered together a great assembly of men, women, and children (inuited by the report of them which first saw vs, who as it seemes, had in that time, of purpose dispersed themselues into the country, to make knowne the newes) who came now the second time vnto vs, bringing with them as before had beene done, feathers and bagges of *Tobah* for presents, or rather indeed for sacrifices, vpon this perswasion that we were Gods.

When they came to the top of the hill, at the bottome whereof wee had built our fort, they made a stand; where one (appointed as their cheife speaker) wearied both vs his hearers, and himselfe too, with a long and tedious oration: deliuered with strange and violent gestures, his voice being extended to the vttermost strength of nature, and his words falling so thicke one in the neck of another, that he could hardly fetch his breath againe: so soone as he had concluded, all the rest, with a reuerend bowing of their bodies (in a dreaming manner, and long producing of the same) cryed *Oh*: thereby giuing their consents, that all was very true which he had spoken, and that they had vttered their minde by his mouth vnto vs; which done, the men laying downe their bowes vpon the hill, and leauing their women and children behinde them, came downe with their presents; in such sort, as if they had appeared before a God indeed: thinking themselues happy, that they might haue accesse vnto our generall, but much more happy, when they sawe that he would receiue at their hands, those things which they so willingly had presented: and no doubt, they thought themselues neerest vnto God, when they sate or stood next to him: In the meane time the women, as if they had been desperate, vsed vnnaturall violence against themselues, crying and shreeking piteously, tearing their flesh with their nailes from their cheekes, in a monstrous manner, the bloode streaming downe along their brests; besides despoiling the vpper parts of their bodies, of those single couerings they formerly had, and holding their hands aboue their heads, that they might not rescue their brests from harme, they would with furie cast themselues vpon the ground, neuer respecting whether it were cleane or soft, but dashed themselues in this manner on hard stones, knobby, hillocks, stocks of wood, and pricking bushes, or whateuer else lay in their way, itterating the same course againe and againe: yea women great with child, some nine or ten times each, and others holding out till 15. or 16. times (till their strengths failed them) exercised this cruelty against themselues: A thing more grieuous for vs to see, or suffer could we haue holpe it, then trouble to them (as it seemed) to do it.

This bloudie sacrifice (against our wils) beeing thus performed, our Generall with his companie in the presence of those strangers fell to prayers: and by signes in lifting vp our eyes and hands to heauen, signified vnto them, that that God whom we did serue, and whom they ought to worship, was aboue: beseeching God if it were his good pleasure to open by some meanes their blinded eyes; that they might in due time be called to the knowledge of him the true and euerliuing God, and of Iesus Christ whom he hath sent, the salutation of the Gentiles. In the time of such prayers, singing of Psalmes, and reading of certaine Chapters in the Bible, they sate very attentiuely: and obseruing the end at euery pause, with one voice still cryed, Oh, greatly reioycing in our exercises. Yea they tooke such pleasure in our singing of Psalmes, that whensoeuer they resorted to vs, their first request was *Gnaah*, by which they intreated that we would sing.

Our General hauing now bestowed vpon them diuers things, at their departure they restored them all againe; none carrying with him any thing of whatsoeuer hee had receiued, thinking themselues sufficiently enriched and happie, that they had found so free accesse to see vs.

Against the end of three daies more (the newes hauing the while spread it selfe farther, and as it seemed a great way vp into the countrie) were assembled the greatest number of people, which wee could reasonably imagine, to dwell within any conuenient distance round about. Amongst the rest, the king himselfe, a man of goodly stature and comely personage, attended with his guard, of about 100. tall and warlike men, this day, viz. Iune 26. came downe to see vs.

Before his coming, were sent two Embassadors or messengers to our Generall, to signifie that their *Hioh*, that is, their king was comming and at hand. They in the deliuery of their message, the one spake with a soft and low voice, prompting his fellow; the other pronounced the same word by words after him, with a voice more audible: continuing their proclamation (for such it was) about halfe an houre. Which being ended, they by signes made request to our Generall, to send something by their hands to their *Hioh*, or king, as a token that his comming might be in peace. Our Generall willingly satisfied their desire; and they, glad men, made speedy returne to their *Hioh*: Neither was it long before their king (making as princely a shew as possibly he could) with all his traine came forward.

In their comming forwards they cryed continually after a singing manner with a lustie courage. And as they drew neerer and neerer towards vs, so did they more and more striue to behaue themselues with a certaine comelinesse and grauity in all their actions.

✗ In the forefront came a man of a large body and goodly aspect, bearing the Septer or royall mace (made of a certaine kind of blacke wood, and in length about a yard and a halfe) before the king. Whereupon hanged two crownes, a bigger and a lesse, with three chaines of a maruellous length, and often doubled; besides a bagge of the herbe *Tabah*. The crownes were made of knitworke, wrought vpon most curiously with feathers of diuers colours, very artificially placed, and of a formall fashion: The chaines seemed of a bony substance: every linke or part thereof being very little, thinne, most finely burnished, with a hole pierced through the middest. The number of linkes going to make one chaine, is in a manner infinite: but of such estimation it is amongst them, that few be the persons that are admitted to weare the same: and euen they to whom its lawfull to vse them, yet are stinted what number they shall vse; as some ten, some twelue, some twentie, and as they exceed in number of chaines, so are they thereby knowne to be the more honorable personages.

Next vnto him that bare this Scepter, was the king himselfe with his guard about him: His attire vpon his head was a cawle of knitworke, wrought vpon somewhat like the crownes, but differing much both in fashion and perfectnesse of worke; vpon his shoulders he had on a coate of the skins of conies, reaching to his wast: His guard also had each coats of the same shape, but of other skins: some hauing cawles likewise stucke with feathers, or couered ouer with a certaine downe, which groweth vp in the country vpon an herbe, much like our lectuce; which exceeds any other downe in the world for finenesse, and beeing layed vpon their cawles by no winds can be remoued: Of such estimation is this herbe amongst them, that the downe thereof is not lawfull to be worne, but of such persons as are about the king (to whom it is permitted to weare a plume of feathers on their heads, in signe of honour) and the seeds are not vsed but onely in sacrifice to their gods. After these in their order, did follow the naked sort of common people; whose haire being long, was gathered into a bunch behind, in which stuck plumes of feathers, but in the forepart onely single feathers like hornes, euery one pleasing himselfe in his owne deuice.

This one thing was obserued to bee generall amongst them all; that euery one had his face painted, some with white, some with blacke, and some with other colours, euery man also bringing in his hand one thing or another for a gift or present: Their traine or last part of their company consisted of women and children, each woman bearing against her breast a round basket or two, hauing within them diuers things, as bagges of *Tobah*, a roote which they call *Petah*, whereof they make a kind of meale, and either bake it into bread, or eate it raw, broyled fishes like a pilchard; the seed and downe aforenamed, with such like:

Their baskets were made in fashion like a deepe boale, and though the matter were rushes, or such other kind of stuffe, yet was it so cunningly handled, that the most part of them would hold water; about the brimmes they were hanged with peeces of the shels of pearles, and in some places with two or three linkes at a place, of the chaines aforenamed: thereby signifying, that they were vessels wholly dedicated to the onely vse of the gods they worshipped: and besides this, they were wrought vpon with the matted downe of red feathers, distinguished into diuers workes and formes.

In the meane time our Generall hauing assembled his men together (as forecasting the danger, and worst that might fall out) prepared himselfe to stand vpon sure ground, that wee might at all times be ready in our owne defence, if anything should chance otherwise than was looked for or expected.

Wherefore euery man being in a warlike readinesse, he marched within his fenced place, making against their approach a most warlike shew (as he did also at all other times of their resort) whereby if they had beene desperate enemies, they could not haue chosen but haue conceiued terrour and feare, with discouragement to attempt anything against vs, in beholding of the same.

When they were come somewhat neere vnto vs, trooping together, they gaue vs a common or a generall salutation: obseruing in the meane time a generall silence. Whereupon he who bare the Scepter before the king, being prompted by another whom the king assigned to that office, pronounced with an audible and manly voice, what the other spake to him in secret: continuing, whether it were his oration or proclamation, at the least halfe an houre. At the close whereof, there was a common *Amen*, in signe of approbation giuen by euery person: And the king himself with the whole number of men and women (the little children onely remaining behind) came further downe the hill, and as they came set themselues againe in their former order.

And being now come to the foot of the hill and neere our fort, the Scepter bearer with a composed countenance and stately carriage began a song, and answerable thereunto, obserued a kind of measures in a dance: whom the king with his guard and euery other sort of person following, did in like manner sing and daunce, sauing onely the women who danced but kept silence. As they danced they still came on: and our Generall perceiuing their plaine and simple meaning, gaue order that they might freely enter without interruption within our bulwarke: Where after they had entred they yet continued their song and dance a reasonable time: their women also following them with their wassaile boales in their hands, their bodies bruised, their faces torne, their dugges, breasts, and other parts bespotted with bloud, trickling downe from the wounds, which with their nailes they had made before their comming.

After that they had satisfied or rather tired themselues in this manner, they made signes to our Generall to haue him sit down; Vnto whom both the king and diuers others made seuerall orations, or rather indeed if wee had vnderstood them, supplications, that hee would take the Prouince and kingdome into his hand, and become their king and patron: making signes that they would resigne vnto him their right and title in the whole land and become his vassals in themselues and their posterities: Which that they might make vs indeed beleeue that it was their true meaning and intent; the king himselfe with all the rest with one consent, and with great reueuerence, ioyfully singing a song, set the crowne vpon his head; inriched his necke with all their chaines; and offering vnto him many other things, honoured him by the name of *Hyoh*. Adding thereunto (as it might seeme) a song and dance of triumph; because they were not onely visited of the gods (for so they still iudged vs to be) but the great and chiefe god was now become their god, their king and patron, and themselues were become the onely happie and blessed people in all the world.

These things being so freely offered, our Generall thought not meet to reiect or refuse the same: both for that he would not giue them any cause of mistrust, or disliking of him (that being the onely place, wherein at this present, we were of necessitie inforced to seeke reliefe of many things) and chiefely, for that he knew not to what good end God had brought this to passe, or what honour and profit it might bring to our countrie in time to come.

Wherefore in the name and to the vse of her most excellent majesty, he tooke the scepter crowne and dignity, of the sayd countrie into his hand; wishing nothing more, than that it had layen so fitly for her maiesty to enioy, as it was now her proper owne, and that the riches and treasures thereof (wherewith in the vpland countries it abounds) might with as great conueniency be transported, to the enriching of her kingdome here at home, as it is in plenty to be attained there: and especially, that so tractable and louing a people, as they shewed themselues to be, might haue meanes to haue manifested their most willing obedience the more vnto her, and by her meanes, as a mother and nurse of the Church of *Christ*, might by the preaching of the Gospell, be brought to the right knowledge, and obedience of the true and euerliuing God.

The ceremonies of this resigning, and receiuing of the kingdome being thus performed, the common sort both of men and women, leauing the king and his guard about him, with our generall, dispersed themselues among our people, taking a diligent view or suruey of euery man; and finding such as pleased their fancies (which commonly were the youngest of vs) they presently enclosing them about, offred their sacrifices vnto them, crying out with lamentable shreekes and moanes, weeping, and scratching, and tearing their very flesh off their faces with their nailes, neither were it the women alone which did this, but euen old men, roaring and crying out, were as violent as the women were.

We groaned in spirit to see the power of Sathan so farre preuaile, in seducing these so harmelesse soules, and laboured by all means, both by shewing our great dislike, and when that serued not, by violent with-holding of their hands from that madnesse, directing them (by our eyes and hands lift vp towards heauen) to the liuing God whom they ought to serue; but so mad were they vpon their Idolatry, that forcible with-holding them would not preuaile (for as soone as they could get liberty to their hands againe, they would be as violent as they were before) till such time, as they whom they worshipped, were conueyed from them into the tents, whom yet as men besides themselues, they would with fury and outrage seeke to haue againe.

After that time had a little qualified their madnes, they then began to shew and make knowne vnto vs their griefes and diseases which they carried about them, some of them hauing old aches, some shruncke sinewes, some old soares and canckred vlcers, some wounds more lately receiued, and the like, in most lamentable manner crauing helpe and cure thereof from vs: making signes, that if we did but blow vpon their griefes, or but touched the diseased places, they would be whole.

Their griefes we could not but take pitty on them, and to our power desire to helpe them: but that (if it pleased God to open their eyes) they might vnderstand we were but men and no gods, we vsed ordinary meanes, as, lotions, emplaisters, and vnguents most fitly (as farre as our skills could guesse) agreeing to the natures of their griefes, beseeching God, if it made for his glory, to giue cure to their diseases by these meanes. The like we did from time to time as they resorted to vs.

Few were the dayes, wherein they were absent from vs, during the whole time of our abode in that place: and ordinarily euery third day, they brought their sacrifices, till such time, as they certainely vnderstood our meaning, that we tooke no pleasure, but were displeased with them: whereupon their zeale abated, and their sacrificing, for a season, to our good liking ceased; notwithstanding they continued still to make their resort vnto vs in great abunddance, and in such sort, that they oft-times forgate, to prouide meate for their owne sustenance: so that our generall (of whom they made account as of a father) was faine to performe the office of a father to them, relieuing them with such victualls, as we had prouided for our selues, as, Muscels, Seales, and such like, wherein they tooke exceeding much content; and seeing that their sacrifices were displeasing to vs, yet (hating ingratitude) they sought to recompence vs, with such things as they had, which they willingly inforced vpon vs, though it were neuer so necessarie or needfull for themselues to keepe.

They are a people of a tractable, free, and louing nature, without guile or treachery; their bowes and arrowes (their only weapons, and almost all their wealth) they vse very skillfully, but yet not to do any great harme with them, being by reason of their weakenesse, more fit for children then for men, sending the arrow neither farre off, nor with any great force: and yet are the men commonly so strong of body, that that, which 2. or 3. of our men could hardly beare, one of them would take vpon his backe, and without grudging carrie it easily away, vp hill and downe hill an English mile together: they are also exceeding swift in running, and of long continuance; the vse whereof is so familiar with them, that they seldom goe, but for the most part runne. One thing we obserued in them with admiration: that if at any time, they chanced to see a fish, so neere the shoare, that they might reach the place without swimming, they would neuer, or very seldome misse to take it.

After that our necessary businesses were well dispatched, our generall with his gentlemen, and many of his company, made a journy vp into the land, to see the manner of their dwelling, and to be the better acquainted, with the nature and commodities of the country. Their houses were all such as wee haue formerly described, and being many of them in one place, made seuerall villages here and there. The inland we found to be farre different from the shoare, a goodly country, and fruitful soyle, stored with many blessings fit for the vse of man: infinite was the company of very large and fat Deere, which there we sawe by thousands, as we supposed, in a heard: besides a multitude of a strange kind of Conies, by farre exceeding them in number: their heads and bodies, in which they resemble other Conies, are but small; his tayle like the tayle of a Rat, exceeding long; and his feet like the pawes of a Want or Moale; vnder his chinne, on either side, he hath a bagge, into which he gathereth his meate, when he hath filled his belly abroade, that he may with it, either feed his young, or feed himselfe, when he lifts not to trauaile from his burrough: the people eate their bodies, and make great account of their skinnes, for their kings holidaies coate was made of them.

This country our generall named *Albion*, and that for two causes; the one in respect of the white bancks and cliffes, which lie toward the sea: the other, that it might haue some affinity, euen in name also, with our owne country, which was sometime so called.

Before we went from thence, our generall caused to be set vp, a monument of our being there; as also of her maiesties, and successors right and title to that kingdome, namely, a plate of brasse, fast nailed to a great and firme post; whereon is engrauen her graces name, and the day and yeare of our arriuall there, and of the free giuing vp, of the prouince and kingdome. both by the king and people, into her maiesties hands: together with her highnesse picture, and armes in a piece of sixpence currant English monie, shewing it selfe by a hole made of purpose through the plate: vnderneath was likewise engrauen the name of our generall &c.

The Spaniards neuer had any dealing, or so much as set a foote in this country; the vtmost of their discoueries, reaching onely to many degrees Southward of this place.

And now, as the time of our departure was perceiued by them to draw nigh, so did the sorrowes and miseries of this people, seeme to themselues to increase vpon them; and the more certaine they were of our going away, the more doubtfull they shewed themselues, what they might doe; so that we might easily iudge that that ioy (being exceeding great) wherewith they receiued vs at our first arriuall, was cleane drowned in their excessiue sorrow for our departing: For they did not onely loose on a sudden all mirth, ioy, glad countenance, pleasant speeches, agility of body, familiar reioycing one with another, and all pleasure what euer flesh and bloud might bee delighted in, but with sighes and sorrowings, with heauy hearts and grieued minds, they powred out wofull complaints and moanes, with bitter teares and wringing of their hands, tormenting themselues. And as men refusing all comfort, they onely accounted themselues as cast-awayes, and those whom thc gods were about to forsake: So that nothing we could say or do, was able to ease them of their so heauy a burthen, or to deliuer them from so desperate a straite, as our leauing of them did seeme to them that it would cast them into.

Howbeit seeing they could not still enjoy our presence, they (supposing vs to be gods indeed) thought it their duties to intreate vs that being absent, we would yet be mindfull of them, and making signes of their desires, that in time to come wee would see them againe, they stole vpon vs a sacrifice, and set it on fire erre we were aware; burning therein a chaine and a bunch of feathers. We laboured by all meanes possible to withhold or withdraw them but could not preuaile, till at last we fell to prayers and singing of Psalmes, whereby they were allured immediately to forget their folly, and leaue their sacrifice vnconsumed, suffering the fire to go out, and imitating vs in all our actions; they fell a lifting vp their eyes and hands to heauen as they saw vs do.

The 23. of Iuly they tooke a sorrowfull farewell of vs, but being loath to leaue vs, they presently ranne to the tops of the hils to keepe vs in their sight as long as they could, making fires before and behind, and on each side of them, burning therein (as is to be supposed) sacrifices at our departure.

Not farre without this harborough did lye certain Ilands (we called them the Ilands of Saint Iames) hauing on them plentifull and great store of Seales and birds, with one of which wee fell Iuly 24. whereon we found such prousion as might serue our turne for a while.

PLATES

PLATE 18

a. Three California Indians from San Francisco pictured by Chamisso, 1822.

b. "Feather bundle" of the Pomo Indians, similar to that described by Fletcher on June 17, 1579.

c. Strings of clamshell disk beads identifiable as the "chaines" of Fletcher.

a

b

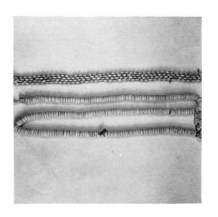

c

PLATE 19

Pomo Indian feathered baskets decorated with clamshell disk beads and abalone shell pendants.

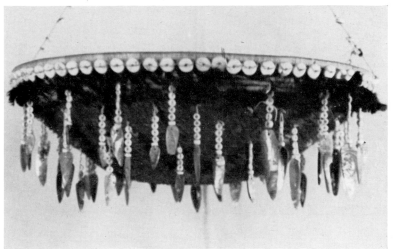

PLATE 20

Air photo of the east cape of Point Reyes. The white dot marks the point selected by George Davidson as the spot where Drake careened the *Golden Hinde*. The shore line of the bay follows the course of the curved arrow.

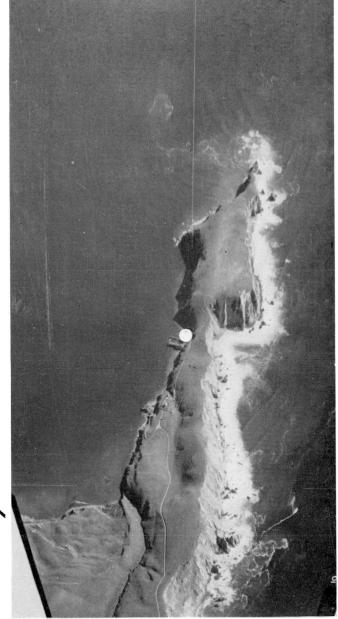

N

PLATE 21

Air photo of the small valley at Drake's Bay, showing the location
(marked near center by white dot) where the Drake plate was found
by William Caldeira in 1934.